I Had a
Preemie
but Now, I Have a
Micro-Preemie!!

Written by Traci Anne Holmes

Order this book online at www.trafford.com or email orders@trafford.com

Most Trafford titles are also available at major online book retailers.

Note for Librarians: A cataloguing record for this book is available from Library
and Archives Canada at www.collectionscanada.ca/amicus/index-e.html

Printed in Victoria, BC, Canada.

ISBN: 978-1-4269-1736-3 (sc)

Trafford rev. 9/21/2009

www.trafford.com

North America & international
toll-free: 1 888 232 4444 (USA & Canada)
phone: 250 383 6864 ♦ fax: 812 355 4082

I have written this book for my three perfect children, CJ, Rana, and Heidi. Also my husband Chris for keeping our family afloat, my parents for running my household and driving me around. Liza and her Dad for being there. Father Allen and all who prayed for Heidi. There are so many more angels that I send my thanks to.

This book is also a dedication to all of the babies in NICUs worldwide being strong and fighting, and their parents who are by their sides.

Lastly, to all of the NICU staff, your job is one of the hardest and you do it for the babies! Thank you.

Here I am in the hospital for the third time fighting to keep my baby inside and here comes the pouring in of phone calls of people who were preemies, have had preemies, or know someone who has had a preemie, all with the same sentiment: "I know how you feel.". I released my resentment of this years ago after my first preemie but here I was in my 23rd week with Obstetricians and Neonatologists now talking to me about IF my baby survives the life of a "micro-preemie" is a scary, unpredictable, roller coaster ride that does not always have a happily ever after story.

Micro-preemie? I am a registered nurse and never in school did I hear this term. I have already had one preemie, fought for my second child to keep her to term and now this, completely unknown territory.

At 25 weeks, I now know what a micro-preemie is. The fight she fought (and won!). How everything goes wrong in the blink of an eye, watching and for months not being able to hold, midnight calls from a nurse about something gone wrong and this is what has to be done..Is it ok?! Moreover, how very few can say they know how I feel!

Having said all of this, I want to tell my story. Every mom of a baby born early has their own story. Mine turns out good, but it was not easy!

The point is I hope to help at least one mom from another who has really been there that the feelings they are having are ok. There is more then a preemie or micro-preemie being brought into your life, there is your life, your emotions, and the just how alone and helpless you feel.

And yes wanting to scream at that kind person who truly is just trying to help by saying they know how you feel because they have, were, or know a preemie, is also perfectly normal!

I owe my life and the life of my micro-preemie to a best friend, her father, and a wonderful doctor. The vital first days of this nightmare would have turned out very different if not for these people.

This is not to say others did not play a vital role in this. My family, minister, a team of doctors and nurses, and three different

NICUs, I have many people who believed and did everything in their power for us.

I thought life would never be the same after my first child was born nine weeks early. Then I had to fight, with myself, to keep my second child inside to be born on time. However, as for my micro-preemie, even with everything done to help her live, she is strong and a fighter. At 15 ounces and 12 inches she didn't appear strong or even alive but her story is that of strength and shear will, of her own, to survive, against all odds! These babies, as I witnessed in the next 18 weeks are strong. Some do not make it, I saw that to but even those babies did not go without a fight!

I hope my story can be an inspiration to anyone going through this or even those that have been through this and still hold on to the emotions.

Contents

Chapter 1

Terms

These words I will be using frequently in my book, especially when I get to the story of my micro-preemie. The terms are defined by me using my medical knowledge and through my times spent in different Neonatal Intensive Care Units (NICUs), unless I have cited another source.

Preemie: any baby born before 37 weeks gestation and weighing less than 2500 grams or 5 ½ pounds.

Micro-preemie: I have heard and seen two definitions.

1. Any baby born before 26 weeks gestation weighing between 700 and 800 grams or 1 ½ pounds.
2. Any baby born before 29 weeks gestation weighing less than 1500 grams or 3 pounds

Preeclampsia: During pregnancy the woman develops hypertension, headaches, swelling of her arms and legs, and protein in the urine.

Placental Abruption: The separation of the placenta from the uterus causing severe bleeding with possible death of the baby and mother.

IUGR: Intrauterine growth retardation: decrease rate of growth of the fetus. This can be a result of any condition that interferes with the blood supply to or state of health of the placenta or the health and general nutrition of the mother. Taber's Cyclopedic Medical Dictionary, Edition 17, F.A. Davis

Bradycardia (Brady): In a preemie or micro-preemie, this is a heart rate below 100 beats per minute.

Desaturation (desat): Is when the oxygen level gets to low, below 90%.

CPAP (Continuous Positive Air Pressure): keeps the air open by giving a constant stream of air.

Sepsis: infection in the blood.

NEC (Necrotizing Enterocolitis): A severe disease of the GI tract of the newborn, esp. the premature. Etiology unknown and treatment is vigorous and symptomatic. The death rate may be as high as 50%. Taber's Cyclopedic Medical Dictionary. Edition 17, F.A. Davis

CHAPTER 2

ME

Before I can tell you of my three pregnancies, I feel I should tell you a little about me. I feel this is important because some women know they could have problems in pregnancy. Some women do not get the care they need for whatever reason, and some women are perfectly healthy and have the worst and most unexpected problems.

I am adopted, not a problem. I had the best life and two of the most loving parents anyone could ever ask for! However, my parents were only given a small piece of my medical history that was provided by my biological mother to social services so life is truly a mystery. I was a full term baby with no complications at birth. I weighed a little over 9 pounds and was 20 inches long. I went right into foster care while waiting for my wonderful parents to come along, when I was 5 months old. While in foster care, I was only a few days old, I stopped breathing, my foster mom rushed me to the ER saving my life.

I had pneumonia at 3 years old, all the colds and flu's of a normal childhood. I developed Migraine headaches when I was 9 years old. One attribute singling me out from my peers was I was (and still am) the clumsiest person ever. I have broken almost every bone in my body and most of which happened from tripping over my own feet.

Medically speaking I had severe migraine headaches and I started my period when I was 10 years old. Yes, I was young and that was hard enough but the problem was I got my period every two weeks for almost two weeks, with a heavy flow. My doctor started me on birth control pills by 12 years old because I was becoming anemic. It took almost 3 years of trying different pills stopping and starting but finally I was controlled enough.

I developed hypothyroidism after my first child but that was easily controlled. I also do not sleep. I have been an insomniac since puberty and I have been on all of the sleep medications out. I have just stopped taking pills and I have learned to live on a couple of hours of sleep a night.

My blood type is A-. Since I am RH negative that means if I have a baby that has a positive blood type and our blood mixes, my body could have an "allergic reaction" to the baby. I have to get a shot mid pregnancy and within 3 days after birth so if my baby has a positive blood type no harm is done to the baby or me.

Ironically, I have always had below average blood pressures. Growing up my blood pressures ranged low 90/60s. While I was a volunteer EMT, I was frequently used for practice because no one could ever say 120/80 with me. Also having to do with my heart, my total cholesterol is so good it is considered to be in the protective range. This is probably what saved my life later on.

All and all I am a healthy person. At 21, my husband and I began dating, I finished college and became a Registered Nurse, I got a wonderful job, and unexpectedly a letter came in the mail. The man who signed me over, as his daughter, for adoption and wanted to find me had contacted Maryland Social Services.

WOW. Always being interested on genetically who I was I called. My mom always supported me and helped anyway she could. She sat next to me and wrote questions for me to ask as I could barely speak without my voice trembling. We met in Florida where he lived, where my future in laws also lived, and as much as we got along there was no way possible he could have been my biological father. This was a huge disappointment as he was a wonderful person, his family was very welcoming, and I had a piece of medical history I could relate to myself.

After a DNA confirmation, he helped me find my biological mother. This was not easy and I could write a whole other book of this experience. I tried for months to contact her and could not. One of my brother's phone numbers was found. I called him and after a lot of, I will call it confusion, I now know my biological mother, 2 sisters, 2 brothers and all of their families. No father. Nevertheless, I have half, right.

My biological mom has not much medically speaking. All of my siblings have told me of them suffering from Headaches, one brother more then the rest. We all have allergies.

One point both of my sisters made is they, including our mother, carry babies to term and some more. No one has had problems during pregnancy.

My biological mothers' parents lived into their 80s. Hypertension, diabetes, and dementia being their primary problems. Between six Aunts and Uncles 1 had leukemia but is ok now and an Aunt has emphysema and most have hypertension.

My oldest sister was diagnosed with Breast Cancer at 43 years old. When she went in for testing on the first lump, they found it was cancer but she also had a form of breast cancer that did not form lumps and was very aggressive. On ultrasound they found new changes in her other breast and life being of the most importance she had a double mastectomy. She is now Cancer free!

CHAPTER 3

Baby #1

Now, I am 24 years old, married and expecting my first baby, a boy. I guess I should have expected things to be different because remember as I said earlier I had been on the pill for most of my life to control my periods well I will say it again, I was expecting my first child! My husband and our parents accepted this way better then I did at first.

I was still taking the pill and my periods were irregular again. I went to the doctor and she was going to do an exploratory laparoscopy to see if there were "structural problems". When the preoperative labs came back pregnant, I could not believe it! I stopped the pill of course and there in an ultrasound was a little shape with a beating heart. I had a period for four months.

My due date was December 6.

What I did not have were my migraines. My migraine headaches went away for the first two pregnancies! That was fabulous, a migraine feels as though my head is being drilled through from the inside out making me sick to my stomach and sensitive to any light.

Half way through my pregnancy, I felt funny. I felt as though I was leaking fluid. I told my doctors who assured me all was well and increased discharge is normal as pregnancy progresses. They did check me and sent me for non-stress tests, again I am told all is well. We set up the date for me to go into the hospital and have the shot for my RH factor. I talked with my sisters but they assured me in our family we not only carry to term but over 40 weeks.

I spoke with one of my best friends to. She had her first child in 1996 and he was born at 28 weeks, her problem was an incompetent cervix. We went through a few pregnancy books and they to stated an increase in discharge was normal.

Therefore, I continued life as normal. I went to work, doctors visits and slowly (but not fast enough) prepared for my first baby.

September 11, 2001. My husband is a Washington DC firefighter and as we woke up that morning, turned on the TV, there it was planes taken over and we all know what happened next. My husband had to go, to the Pentagon. For the next three days, I heard nothing from him. I tried to stay calm and remember that even though everyone has assured me I was all right I still felt something was wrong. How could I be so selfish thinking of me when so many lives have been permanently altered and where was my husband? After my husband was home, I spent my time worrying about him. He was not the man I married and never would be again. How could he after the things he had seen and will never forget. I continued working and going to my doctor appointments as I should but I stopped complaining about something that I was obviously wrong about.

October 3.

When my husband worked, I did not like being home alone so I would spend the nights at my parents' house. I worked 15 hours and just wanted to go to bed. I went to sleep easily which was very unusual for me, an insomniac. I woke up with a feeling of pure terror.

Midnight, my dog who slept curled up next to me soaking wet. What was going on? Was I sleeping so hard I peed myself? I got out of bed and as soon as I was able to stand up, another gush of water all over the floor. I called the on call doctor and after waiting 20 minutes, which felt like an hour, the doctor assured me it was probably an "accident" as I originally thought but I should go to the hospital. My heart was pounding, I was terrified to move but I woke my mom up and she took me to the hospital.

On the Labor and Delivery unit a very nice nurse took us to a small examine room and told us being my first baby and I was young I was fine and women do have accidents and not to be embarrassed. I was to put on a gown for an examination but "relax". The nurse turned to walk out as I stood up and yet again an enormous gush of water everywhere.

The good news was finally someone believed me that something was wrong. The bad news is I am only 30 almost 31 weeks along. After a lot of shuffling me into a labor and delivery room, monitors, blood work and exams, my water did break, I was 3 cm dilated, with contractions (I did not feel) every 4 minutes. The biggest question now is how long they can postpone delivery.

It was 5am before my husband was called and he went back to sleep. He told me "oh ok I'll see you later, love you" before realizing what I had just told him. I had to call back and tell the firefighter who answered the phone what was happening so he could get Chris up. He came from the firehouse and did not leave my side until he and I could go home together.

This is when all of the very kind but not helpful for me people began with everything will be fine. I was, I have had, or I know of...a preemie.

I was put on continuous monitoring, given the first of three steroid injections for the babies underdeveloped lungs and now we wait. An ultrasound showed the baby was big for my gestation, may be they were off on my due date. I did not have gestational diabetes! The lung function test they took that first night is back and no, his lungs are not developed, my due date is correct and the baby is just big.

Seven days later, October 11 2001, due to the risk of infection I had to be delivered for both of our sakes. I was induced at 10am.

No one told me the pain of induction is much more intense than the pain of the body's natural labor process. Plus this is my first baby I did not know what to expect naturally. I was not dilating so I was given IV pain medication, several times over a few hours. I was in so much pain I tried all different kinds of repositioning and nothing helped.

Still 3 cm with the Pitocin so high I started to bleed slightly with each contraction. My mom and Chris tried everything to sooth me. Chris and I had attended the first of three Lamaze classes but my water broke before we could finish. Chris was doing what he was instructed to that first night but I wanted to strangle him!

Finally my doctor decided I needed and epidural, even though I wasn't dilated to the point were they do this he was using a theory of get me relaxed and then my body would do as it was supposed to. (This theory worked but the problem was getting into my back).

The anesthesiologist tried three times and could not get the catheter in the right place in my back so he gave me a spinal. The most concerning difference in the two right now is with an epidural they can give me medication for long periods of time, a spinal is a one shot deal and lasts only about 1 hour.

I was finally comfortable, I still could feel the contractions because the Pitocin was still being poured in but it was tolerable. My door opened at 730 pm and a doctor walks in and introduces himself to us. He was there because there were changes on the monitor and he needed to check me, my doctor was gone for the night and he was on call. He barely started his exam when he calmly pressed the emergency button on my bed, not the nurses call button but the emergency button.

Two nurses came in my room and looking at me, he told them the babies' head was crowning and it was time. One of the nurses ran out of the room, she was getting the NICU team, the other nurse scrambled about to get the doctor ready, and the things set up for delivery and the baby warmer.

All of a sudden, there were a dozen people in my room. Most of them went over to the corner of the room were the baby would go and they were turning things on they brought with them and talking among themselves. I could not really pay to much attention because this doctor who was nice enough but I did not know just said my baby was coming.

He told Chris to get his camera if he wanted pictures of the baby. At that point, my mom went to the waiting room, she was more comfortable there. The doctor stayed very close to me while getting himself prepared and kept talking to me, very calmly, but telling me not to push.

Finally, everyone was ready, but me, and all eyes turned to me. I am a very modest person and now a dozen people were looking at me in a not modest position. Three pushes and he was here at 8pm. That part was easier for me then I thought. Chris cut the umbilical cord and followed the NICU nurses over to the warmer snapping a few pictures.

CJ cried right away, and the tears started streaming down my face. I guess the doctor thought that I was worried because he told me that was good but that was why I was crying. CJ crying meant his lungs even premature were ok. I did not get to hold him but they let me peek at him before they took him away.

He seemed well. He weighed 5 lbs 2oz and was 19.5 inches long. Everything WAS going to be ok. They took him away just to look him over and clean him up. I was moved to a postpartum room and told they would let me see him as soon as he was completely checked out.

3 AM my husband and I looked at each other, neither one having slept, and finally called for a nurse. Then we found out he had been in the regular nursery "fine" but started having trouble breathing and could not maintain a warm enough temperature and had to go over to the NICU. "No one let you know?"

I guess to a NICU team delivering a crying 5-pound baby was a great thing and everything was ok. However, despite his size, my son was 9 weeks early and could not breathe well on his own and his brain was not sending the right signals to regulate his body temperature.

My first time seeing him in the NICU was life altering for me. He looked big – enough. He took up almost the entire incubator.

However, he needed oxygen to breath and the heat inside his box to warm him. He had a feeding tube through his nose and several IVs in his arms and legs. I was able to hold him but only for short periods before he was cold. We were told he would be in the hospital for a few weeks to a month.

The worst day was leaving him. Signing my discharge instructions and leaving him in the hospital.

I had several failed epidurals and a spinal and now I suffered from a spinal Headache. I thought my migraines were bad but nothing compared this, my neck actually locked to the side and I could not move it for almost two days.

I was going to pump my milk (which came in 4 days prior to CJs birth) so we had to go and rent the pump on the way home.

This is a terrible experience in so many ways. First that day and the few following I had this spinal headache. My neck locked to the side and everything had to be done for me. We went to rent the pump and being a first time mom, I really did not have a clue. My milk had been leaking and really had come in now, I was already engorged. The women explained the pump and how to store my milk. When we got home and Chris got the pump set up it was terrible. Everything was on low settings so nothing I experienced was from to high suction but it really hurt. I had an over supply of milk. I filled my freezer, the NICUs and my moms.

No one ever tells you that it is not a comfortable experience. Even when CJ was home and nursing when let down occurred it was painful, and I was always engorged. CJ ate and ate well but my body just kept going! I was not so lucky later on.

CHAPTER 4

The NICU

Another thing you are never prepared for is the NICU. I did some of my nursing training at this very hospital, in this unit. But to walk in as the mom of one its patients was a sobering experience.

Not only are you looking at your baby you are surrounded by all of the other babies born early or with another problem fighting their own battles with their scared parents looking over them. Nurses moving quietly about, Doctors in and out, monitors (everywhere) were beeping.

There are a few things after all of my experience with NICUs I want to recommend. I will reinforce this later.

First, start a journal, this way you can write down what you are told, questions you have, and your own feelings and observations.

Secondly, question everything. It is your right to know what is happening to your baby and you can be in the best of NICUs but they are in a routine, they treat infants' day in and day out, they won't tell you everything, not on purpose but because they are so used to this.

Important things to ask no matter if this is your first NICU or your fifth. You want to know the basics, how is the baby today, any changes? If so what and what has been done. Understand the equipment and medications that are for your baby. Ask who the primary doctor is caring for your baby and who to call for information.

The NICU is like a roller coaster. Your baby will have great days, ok days, and horrible days. Ask if you will be notified of changes other than major changes.

Lastly ask what you can do to help with your baby, change a diaper, take a temperature, you will be amazed how just a small thing like one of these will make you feel useful.

Chapter 5

Next

Then adding insult to injury are my hormones. I just had a baby, my body is a mess. But instead of cuddling my newborn baby and nursing him, rocking him to sleep, I am looking at him through a plastic wall, pumping milk, and wanting to cry and scream, but I have to look like I am holding it together so no one worries about me.

My husband has a great ability to shift stress. Do something else to keep your mind busy. He is also an eternal optimist, something I have always admired. I am his polar opposite. I am the eternal pessimist; I will be able to worry myself to death one day.

Everyday I woke up and called to check on my son, CJ. I would get cleaned up and spend my days at the NICU dreading being asked to leave so they could put in a Nasal Gastric Tube (NGT) in him because he won't eat, or a spinal tap for the fever he developed, or it was night now and I had to go home.

During this time, my mother and sister in law threw me a baby shower. This was good because I had very little for him to come home to. This was also another time for people to tell me they knew what I was going through because…. I know every smile I gave looked false but they were. I could not be distracted.

Then the phone rang. I did not think anything of it this is my mother in laws home. It was for me, the hospital. I had told them where I would be if they needed me.

The doctor that day, a new obstetrician in my doctors group, thought since I was gone she would circumcise CJ. Well, they were calling to tell me they were very sorry they did not obtain consent first. Ok I thought we were going to have that done anyway. That was not all. The nurse asked me to hold that the doctor wanted to speak with me. She introduced her self and apologized. FOR?? The silence was deafening. She finally told me that during the procedure she cut the under side of his penis and got a vein. He has seven stitches.

That pretty much ended the baby shower for me; I left and went to the hospital.

What I know no one else understood but what I could not talk to anyone about is my guilt. I felt very responsible for my son being born early. Irrational yes, but how I felt yes.

To me the one and only job I had was to take care of myself there for taking care of my baby and bringing him into this world on time healthy. I failed at my one and only purpose.

After 3 1/2 weeks, CJ came home. Everyone was thrilled. People called, I was told how they were right everything is ok.

I was not thrilled and I was so scared of him. The NICU doing their job put the fear of SIDS in me. For the first two months, CJ was home I slept maybe one hour a night and not all at once. I kept the lights dimmed the TV on, anything to keep me awake so I could watch him and be ready to save him should he stop breathing. I was so tired I actually started hallucinating.

Finally, my husbands work schedule slowed and my mom retired and they would watch him during the day for a short time. I would not let him go. I would take brief naps to energize myself for the night watch.

Then there was the eating and never sleeping, at least not for any length of time. CJ nursed every 2 hours for 30 minutes for over 6 months. I produced so much milk at first we had real problems with him choking. Between my fear of SIDS and his constant eating, I kept CJ in the bed with me.

I know there are critics of this and those that encourage the family bed. I did not care who thought what. He was mine and this worked for us. The part that did not work was the first few months Chris had to sleep in another room. He was scared to be in the bed with CJ because he was a hard sleeper and did not want to hurt him but even when he got a little bigger and Chris did not mind that anymore it was falling asleep with CJ always needing to eat. This was not a serene scene either as I had to turn on lights for CJs choking spells and I always needed to clean myself up. Nursing pads did not work for me, I actually wore preemie diapers.

CJ did have a lot of breathing problems. The pediatricians would not classify it as asthma because he was a baby but we spent a lot of time with his respiratory distress syndrome now asthma. He had some mild GI problems requiring specialists also. Through it all we made it. He became stronger and I regained sanity.

CJ is now 7 years old, he has controlled asthma and developed a seizure disorder this past year but he is a normal happy little boy.

I also understand the saying "Thank God for Little Favors". The doctors estimated CJ would have been near 10 pounds if I carried him to term!

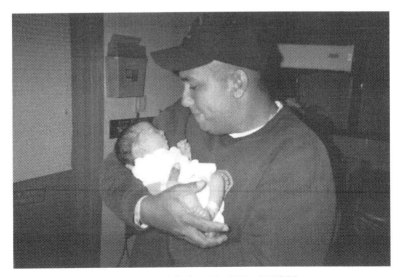

Pictures of dad with CJ in NICU

16

For the first few months after CJ was born I had a hard time losing my baby weight. I was eating healthy and exercising a little (I never exercised prior to having kids). I developed pain in my legs and in my joints mainly my knees, elbows and fingers, my skin became extremely dry and I usually have oily skin. I was so tired but I did not feel that solely due to CJ and my fixation with watching him sleep.

After about 2 months of my OB/GYN telling me this was typical post partum stuff I went to my primary care doctor.

He took one look at me and told me he had a pretty good idea of what was wrong with me but wanted to do blood work and I was to come back in to the office in one week. I was then diagnosed with hypothyroidism.

I was easily adjusted on medication and have not had a problem. My doctor assumed it was my body going through the pregnancy that made me develop this, true or not it is what it is.

CHAPTER 6

Baby #2

Two and half years later, my husband and I decided we were ready to have another baby. I started prenatal vitamins 3 months before we started trying and spoke with my doctor. My doctor assured me that they would watch me closer and there was still no reason for my water breaking with CJ. Being very fertile when we said we wanted another baby, I was pregnant. I still had a period for three months but otherwise "normal".

My prenatal care was much more frequent as the doctor was concerned for a possible incompetent cervix and wanted to be proactive this time around. At 19 weeks, I started to efface (thinning of cervix) but no sign of dilating. I was then put on bed rest.

My husband, Chris, yet again had to spend all of his time working due to us going back to a single income. My mom helped me with CJ and he had a wonderful daycare provider just down the street. She was always very concerned for the baby and me and took extra care of CJ and me.

I had prenatal checkups every two weeks. I did not feel like I had with CJ, there was no "leaking". I actually felt normal but I was worried making yet another pregnancy not enjoyable.

Slowly I fully effaced then by 32 weeks, I started to dilate. I was now being checked twice a week and having non stress tests and ultrasounds almost as frequently.

It was not until my thirteenth ultrasound that the baby revealed she was a girl. I slowly dilated to 4 cm by 35 weeks. No contractions, water in tact. My doctors had no idea why I was not going into labor or how my water was remaining intact with how dilated I was but no one was complaining.

April 29, 2004 I woke up with a nosebleed. No big deal for most people but I have had only one other nose bleed in my life and I had broken my nose for that. Being a nurse, I checked my blood pressure and it was 150/100. I called the doctor and of course was sent to the hospital to be checked for preeclampsia. Chris was home this time and accompanied me to the hospital. I was nervous but I knew I was far enough along this time I was not worried for her.

After a full work up the tests came back negative for preeclampsia but the doctor classified me with PIH (pregnancy-induced hypertension) and decided my pregnancy had gone on long enough and the baby should be delivered.

Again, at 4 cm for two weeks no one really understood why I was not in labor anyway. My doctor had to leave a few hours prior and the labor and delivery staff called the House doctor (a doctor who looks after the whole hospital) to break my water.

Nothing ever being easy with me, the doctor came and said he broke my water, for the sake of not getting to graphic, I was not even dribbling! The nurses reported to my doctor that the House doctor came and I had no change so up went the Pitocin.

Induction really is a terrible thing. On the plus side, I knew what to expect making the pain slightly more bearable.

Two hours (I have been in the hospital for 8 hours now) later at 4 pm my doctor came back and checked me finding my water still intact. She broke my water and the Anesthesia doctors came and between three of them unsuccessfully poked another four holes in my back before I had enough. All was well because when they laid me back down my daughter was trying to make her appearance on her own.

Chris, I still have the picture burned in my mind, looked like he was a statue, pale as a ghost. Now my husband has delivered babies before in houses and ambulances but the thought of it being just him and the nurse he was terrified! That did make me laugh.

My doctor came when the nurse called and quickly said she had to return a call quickly and walked out. Chris and the nurse stared at each other and the nurse went running after her, yelling to me not to push! My Doctor never had enough time to fully get her self together because with an induced contraction Rana came bounding out without any help at all. 7 lbs 12oz, 20 in. Perfectly healthy.

Her second day of life when our pediatrician came to assess her heard a small heart murmur, which kept her in the hospital an extra day but they let me stay to so we all went home together this time.

Rana is a happy and healthy child. Her murmur went away within weeks. We all have allergy-induced asthma but that is no big thing and well controlled. She also has had chronic ear infections leading to some speech problems.

However, we found the best Speech Therapist and even before getting PE tubes (ear tubes) put in, Rana was improving. This Speech Therapist was also very warm and loving to Rana and our family, making us meals and offering to keep Rana some during everything with Baby #3. Rana was also my best baby at home so far.

CJ never slept for any length of time. He was up and wanted to be nursed every two hours and he did this for months. Everyone thought once he started cereal and other foods at six months he would get better but even now, at 7 years old he has trouble sleeping. He is my son.

Rana on the other hand is her father. Chris can sleep standing up. He just closes his eyes and away he goes. At six days old Rana slept through the night. I woke up scared to death something was wrong and woke her that first night but then was instructed to never wake a sleeping baby.

Rana went to bed at 830 pm and slept until 7 am. She was fabulous! I had the same trouble with my milk being in high supply but Rana was able to empty each breast in a feeding.

However with her sleeping through the night, and I was not pumping, I had to keep diapers in my bra again and a towel under me to catch the rest. The first feeding of the day was very painful from the engorgement.

I did start her on formula at 6 months old. We decided we needed a bigger home and were in the process of moving and this made it easier. CJ, I nursed for a full year, he never had a taste of formula.

Picture of baby Rana

Chapter 7
2005-2006

With two now perfect children, a boy and girl, we are done. Pregnancy is no fun for me and always worrying does not help. However…

2005-2006

The area both Chris and I grew up in had changed and not for the good. It was no longer safe and we did not want to risk harm to our children.

We moved away and this meant we needed new doctors. I was lucky enough to find an OB/GYN I liked even though I was done having babies, over the next few years I had a lot of menstrual problems.

My periods were so heavy I went through a pack of pads in a few days. I finally went to the doctor embarrassed for even worrying after all these years and I finally had the exploratory lap.

Interestingly I had a moderate amount of endometriosis. Now this usually makes it very hard for women to have children. My doctor fixed me up and life went on. We are now using "natural" birth control methods.

In September of 2005, I injured my back at work and I had to have surgery to remove a herniated disc. I also have two other discs that have degenerated and could go anytime.

January 17, 2006, I had the surgery and spent the next six weeks getting back on my feet. Chris was studying for is promotional exam while trying to keep up with two toddlers and admittedly I was very stubborn and did not like all of my exercises which he made me do.

My parents came over everyday and a close friend that has since moved on took the kids out, just to get them out.

One of the rules after back surgery is no children. The stress of weight is not good and epidurals and spinals may not be successful. Ha! I already know that one. We were done so no big deal.

In March, I developed pneumonia and fluid in my chest. I had to have a thoracentisis (sticking a needle into my back and draining the fluid). Rana and CJ both also spent a week each this year in the hospital with pneumonia.

CHAPTER 8

Baby #3

June 2007, we are getting ready for vacation and I was packing. I am very meticulous, making lists for each member of the family so nothing is forgotten.

That was when I learned what was forgotten, my period. This was nothing I have ever forgotten but it was not there. I ran to the store bought three different brands of pregnancy tests and all three told me our family was growing and this was going to be the biggest challenge yet.

I was very upset, angry is more of the appropriate term. I did not want to be pregnant, I was scared to death of being pregnant, and I should not have gotten pregnant! By the time I started getting excited about having another baby disaster struck and my emotional state went right out the window.

My due date was February 29 2008.

The OB/GYN I have come to trust and really liked retired from Obstetrics. Living in a small town there were not a lot of choices. I did my research looking at my town, and three other towns that were about 40 minutes away that our insurance used.

I talked to a few other women I knew and of there experiences and made a choice of the one doctor who all around was highly regarded. I was scared because I had come to really trust my other now GYN only.

I lived to far to go back to my old doctors though I wasn't sure I would do that any how so I made a leap and trusted the words I had been given by many. I knew my old doctor and the doctor I would return to after the baby would be on call at the community hospital in my town so that also comforted me.

With my history, the new doctor and I agreed I needed to be watched closely. Not having gone through my two other pregnancies with me he questioned the possibility of incompetent cervix and preeclampsia not buying the PIH diagnosis I was given before. I had frequent visits and cervical checks.

There was a big difference from the very start that should have alerted me. My migraine headaches never went away! In fact, I think they were worse, more frequent with more intensity.

By the middle of summer, and I am only a few months along, I stayed in my dark bedroom so I would not be sick. I missed a whole summer with CJ and Rana. CJ learned how to ride his bike this summer. Rana just enjoyed the out doors, chasing butterflies and coloring on the driveway.

At 19 weeks, I had my first sonogram. I was told I had healthy baby girl weighing approximately 1 pound, with no signs of effacing. This was wonderful news to me. The doctor felt we could have fewer visits and planned on a new test that could tell him if I was at risk for going into labor but I had to be 25 weeks before having the test. Maybe this pregnancy would be better than then the second, which had turned out better than the first.

For the next two weeks I actually did very little worrying. I had two children to care for a job and a husband whose career was taking off. Chris is now a certified K9 handler and he and his dog work for FEMA helping find those in need, like Hurricanes, collapses, ECT. Everything is going to be ok.

I started to have swelling in my hands and feet around my 21st week. I had headaches that would not go away not even for a short time. This is significantly different from either pregnancy. Alarms are now ringing in my head. I take my blood pressure and it is 110/90. My diastolic is getting high, other than when I woke up with that nosebleed that led to the birth of Rana I have a low blood pressure. My average blood pressures through my life were 90s/60s.

I called and went to see the doctor. His nurse took my blood pressure saying it was fine. I knew she was wrong. I told him about my readings and I had swollen hands and feet. He did an ultrasound and he said the baby was fine, my cervix was fine, and I was fine.

This is where my guilt starts. I left that office and did not fight for my baby or myself. I knew he was wrong, I knew I needed to start medication for my blood pressure but I left.

Being a nurse, especially in the career I have had, patient advocacy was a big deal for me. I have stood up to doctors hundreds of times and some of those for lesser reasons than I had right now. I did not advocate for me, for my baby girl. Guilt is a terrible thing. Many people feel guilty about things they could not control but the feelings are there and people telling you, you should not feel guilty makes it worse.

Saturday, November 3, 2007, Chris has left for K9 training and my parents are out of town too. I had such a severe headache that every time my kids made a noise I was sick and the flashes of light in my eyes were even scarier. I took my blood pressure and there on the monitor it said 160/106. NO WAY. I took it again and it got slightly higher. I called my doctor and my old doctor was on call. Thank god, now I will be taken care of.

My next problem. How was I going to go to the hospital and watch my kids? I called several neighbors and one close friend. This friend turns out to be my godsend and Baby #3s godmother. She literally saved our lives.

I called her and got voice mail. At that point, I decided I would wait until Monday and just spend as much time as possible in bed on my left side and pray everyone would be ok-very foolish thinking again. My friend called me about half an hour later and I told her what was happening but if she could watch my kids I would drive myself to the hospital and get checked out. I could barely see and threw up at even the lowest sounds.

She saw me, threw me in her van and dropped me at the hospital. Little did I know I was not coming out with my baby?

Liza took my kids, called Chris and my parents, and had her dad come to be with me. Liza's dad is my next lifesaver. If her dad had not have come I think I would have lost my mind! I was now in the Labor and Delivery unit of very small community hospital.

There is no NICU and the staff that has been there forever is not trained to care for premature babies.

My doctor met me at the hospital. With Liza's dad by side IVs and lab work were being done. With my blood pressure getting higher my doctor personally gave me the IV medication we prayed would work, and stayed at my bedside until the maximum dose was given. After the maximum amount was given to me, my blood pressure though still high stopped rising.

I went down for an ultrasound. The shocking news I received there was my baby, my daughter, was less than a pound. Less than a month ago for my first ultrasound I was told the baby was 1 pound and growing. They do not shrink so I now was told the baby was not growing due to my blood pressure also known as intrauterine growth retardation (IUGR).

Back to the Maternity unit I am now being put on strict bed rest with Magnesium being tapered up to what will soon be such a high dose I loose my sight and control of my legs. I also have a Foley catheter put in so they can collect my urine to positively conclude the diagnosis of preeclampsia not to mention I cannot use my legs.

It is explained to me that if my blood pressure is not gotten in hand and I have to have my baby she will die. I am 23 weeks and she is less than 1 pound. No Chance for Survival!

My parents came in sometime that night beating my husband. My mom stayed the night with me and my husband made it the next morning (in time to see me fly). My children were able to come for a short visit but CJ, 6, got very scared seeing me unable to see. I reached to where I thought I was seeing him for a hug and I was way off. Rana, 3, just did not understand.

My doctor came in during the night and called frequently to check on me. The next morning things got worse. The urine they did have was sent for testing because I was now on the highest doses of magnesium, my blood pressure was now 170s/110s, when I really rested and was on my left side we could get down to 150/100s.

The protein in my urine came back at 10 grams (there should be none or very little protein in your urine). My doctor than made the decision that if my baby and me for that matter had a chance of survival I needed the care of a much better facility.

I was given the option of two hospitals. One I was not familiar with even though its reputation was good and it was a little closer to home, the second was known worldwide and I had some experience there. It was a city hospital making the drive for my family a bit further but I wanted the best chance for my baby's life so I choose the known.

It was also decided a 2-hour ambulance ride plus the time for a private ambulance to get to me was out so I was to be flown a 15-minute journey to the next phase of my nightmare.

Due to the high doses of Magnesium and probably just good old stress, I do not remember everything that happened to me until a few days after my baby was torn out of me. I will continue with what I remember and things Chris and my mom have told me.

CHAPTER 9

Transfer to JH

November 4, 2007

From the time it was decided I had to be flown, the helicopter was there in 20 minutes. My minister came in and prayed for us as the flight nurse and medic prepared me. Chris came in as they were wheeling me out of the room. It was only a 15-minute flight but I remember being terrified, I was alone, my baby could die, and so could I.

The one thing I remember, very clearly, is the flight medic holding my hand from the time we were in the helicopter to the time we touched down at the new hospital. He did not try to talk me out of my tears or cheer me up he just held my hand.

20 minutes have now passed since I left my small town and my family. I am now surrounded by loud noises and a blur of people all talking to each other, me, I cannot see. People talking, touching, no one explaining, no one was introducing themselves. Its ok I am in the city and the important thing is my care, my baby's life.

I do not know when as time is concerned but eventually things calmed, voices became quieter and more familiar and soon there were only a few. I was in a room, I had IVs, monitors for the baby and my heart stuck all over. Finally I am understanding I have filled out admission forms, given my medical history, been seen by a team of doctors and students (this is a teaching hospital), and now a plan of care has been set in action.

I was still being given the Magnesium and now more IV blood pressure medication. My head is still throbbing, nothing to undo stress like a constant grinding headache. Chris gets to the hospital sometime in the afternoon.

We are now informed of the plan. Another 24 hour urine is to be completed (this will wind up being the second of four I have), IV medication will be given in set intervals until a blood pressure of acceptable high is maintained. Another sonogram is to be performed to gage the baby's weight. Tests to see if there is another cause like Autoimmune could be doing this, and the last of the three steroid injections for the babies lungs (I had one at my home hospital and one when I arrived at the new hospital).

Above all bed rest for hopefully a few weeks (months) so the baby can get bigger and stronger. No one ever expected me to carry to term but we were hoping for at least four weeks.

I was stabilized to a blood pressure of 150s/110s, Taken off of the Magnesium (yeah I can see!) and moved to a quiet room on the maternity unit so all the other tests could be done. This is to be my resting place until the birth.

Chris and my parents came to visit when they could but I insisted on some normalcy for CJ and Rana. CJ had school and Rana had preschool all good support systems I wanted them to have. Chris had to work. We knew now we were facing financial hardship as I was going to be out of work for what is now almost two years.

My vital signs were monitored every two hours around the clock. Just the stress of someone coming in and flicking on lights in the middle night shot my blood pressure up. Doctors, Interns, students came and went from all specialties. I had sonograms of my kidneys and an echocardiogram of my heart.

The sonogram of my baby remained of the highest concern, as they cannot offer a perfect reading they would approximate high for her birth weight and give her 1.5 pounds or 500 grams. This was necessary as the NICU was always on alert for her birth.

Grams not pounds are what these tiny babies are weighed in, mainly for medication purposes.

Rheumatology ran their tests and although I had markers for an autoimmune disease they did not know which one and felt sure this was not the cause.

A renal doctor wanted to do a kidney biopsy feeling they could definitely find out the problem but I refused I needed no more pain to raise my BP and it was now obvious to me I had preeclampsia hanging very near the end of that diagnosis to full Eclampsia.

November 7, 2007,

Being on bed rest for what was hoped to be along period they allowed me bathroom privileges. I woke up that morning prepared to add to my third 24-hour urine sample and I was bleeding. I very literally felt my blood pressure rise.

I was taken back over to the labor and delivery side for IV medication again and fetal monitoring. One of the two doctors I had this day came in and tried to easy my anxiety by thinking the bleeding was caused by a previous exam and I was no longer bleeding. I was then told "oh but by the way, you are now 2 cm dilated."

For the love of all that is holy, what else is going to go wrong?

Chris arrived quickly after the call that I was bleeding. My minister also arrived hoping to give me some hope. This is when we had our first visit from a Neonatologist. She was there to tell us what to expect if my baby was born now at 24 weeks with a hopeful birth weight of 1.5 pounds.

This was one of those talks that you never want hear. She started from the baby's brain and worked her way down the body of all the possible problems/complications that could and probably would happen, and again that is if she even survives. There is also a Preemie book that is given to you once your baby has made it to the NICU that goes through the same outline.

The next two days I spent being watched closely, everyone waiting for the sign for either me to have to be a complete emergency, for the baby or me. I spent my time talking to my kids on the phone for a few minutes each day and trying to deep breath and relax. Was that even possible?

CHAPTER 10

The DAY

November 10 2007

I woke this morning very happy. I felt no worse but the best thing was about to happen. My mom was bringing my kids to visit me. Chris has to work so she spends the days and nights he is gone with them. I was allowed into the bathroom to finally finish, the fourth and final, 24-hour urine and that was whisked away to the lab. Later I find out it sat outside my room until 2pm.

I cleaned up the best I could not being allowed a bath or shower (yuck)! Now I waited.

A little before 10am my door creaks open a tiny bit. It must be my vital sign time. Then the best vision I could have had at this time was my sons' eyes peeping through the crack at me. When our eyes met he nearly put a whole in the wall by opening the door so fast and he was there, next to my bed holding my hand.

Following behind him a few seconds later was Rana and my mom. Rana ran to other side of the bed and worked her way on to the bed, wiggled through the IV lines and she was then in my arms. For this short place in time, everything was perfect!

Since I was not allowed to sit up, the kids played on the bed or around the room and my mom being as supportive as ever made the visit as long as she could.

It was Saturday and there was little on TV and in a hospital room not much to do. My mom took CJ and Rana to lunch and short walks during my assessments and vital signs.

Then around 230 pm a group of doctors and nurses come into my room. My kids hovered close to me and my mom became very intent on listening. The 24-hour urine that should have been sent hours ago to the lab came back and showed the protein in my urine was over 16 grams. They were very concerned about my health and the baby and wanted to move me again to the labor and delivery unit for monitoring and possible induction.

My mom and kids helped gather some of my things and walked with everyone as I was moved to another room. It was getting late for their two-hour drive home and with no decisions made other than to monitor me my mom and kids said a very tearful goodbye and I watched my children leave.

I should have known something else life altering was going to happen. CJ and Rana had been over to see me a few times and left upset but ok. Not tonight. Rana cried, hard, and CJ had to be pried off of me, both of us crying.

Not more than 20 minutes after they left two new doctors came into my room behind them three nurses. The nurses went to work.

One started yet another IV on me, one was hanging something new to my IV, and the other stayed near the doctors with a clipboard full of papers. The doctors taking turns talking but almost finishing each others sentences informed me that with the protein in my urine being so high and after watching the baby on the monitors for the short time I had been hooked back up I had to be delivered.

A normal delivery is not possible because it could take to long and the baby is too small, they needed to do a C-Section, which turned into an emergency C-Section. I did not want this but I had already assumed that was going to be the only way and had come to terms with it.

They also wanted to start the magnesium back up for my blood pressure and several other reasons that just went in and out of my head.

I was now officially in a state of shock. This was happening, now, and I was 25 weeks 2 days, the baby was too small, too early, and I was alone.

After signing all the paper work for surgery and anesthesia one of the nurses saw I was slowly not keeping it as together as I thought I was. I do not know her name and never saw her face as the Magnesium doing what it did to me, took my sight, she immediately got Chris's phone number and tried calling. After several failed attempts, I asked her to call my mom. She did get her after a few tries and she was going to drop my kids off to my dad and would be back to the hospital as soon as she could. The nurse told her she would not be able to keep trying Chris and mom did get a hold of him.

An hour had passed, and Chris was suddenly there. Out on a fire call he got the message and he raced to get the hospital. What should have been at least an hour and a half took him 45 minutes.

He walked into my room while anesthesia was trying to place an arterial catheter in my wrist. This would give them a better since of a true blood pressure, however with it being higher than ever this was a long and very painful process.

I still bare the six scars on the inside of my left wrist. After the catheter was finally placed, we discussed an epidural. I had met with one of the two that were present before and explained that previous attempts at spinals and epidurals had failed and on top of that, I had had spinal surgery. They felt confident this would not be a problem.

General anesthesia at this point was a very last resort, as the medications would sedate and effect an already compromised baby.

It was now time to go to the Operating Room. Chris was told where to go to change and they would get him very soon. I remember him trying to keep the look on his face positive as he kissed me and told me everything was going to be ok, "see you in a few". Unfortunately, as this whole experience was he did not get to see me soon.

Now in the operating room two new nurses introduced themselves to me. They seemed very confident of what was happening. A group of people passed by me one stopping and introducing herself as the neonatal doctor tonight. They were setting up everything they were going to need to work on my very premature baby.

The anesthesia doctors came next and prepped for my epidural. As I knew, it was a problem. From what I was told by one of the nurses and Chris I passed out during the third attempt and they lost the baby's heartbeat. They were going to put me under general anesthesia but they got the heartbeat back and continued trying for the epidural.

I remember lying on the table with one of the anesthesiologist over my head and one of the operating doctors at my side. They were pinching my right leg and it hurt. They tipped the table so I was laying right side down for a while and pinched my legs and stomach more. I still had feeling on my right side. During this time they finally let Chris back. He said he had been waiting along time and my mom was in the waiting room.

It was determined by the baby's heart it was time. Even with me still having feeling in my right side, she had to be delivered. They made an incision and gave me local anesthetic injections another incision and local anesthetic doing this down to my uterus. This is the single most physically painful thing I have ever felt. Every cut for what seemed like forever.

Through my mumbling trying not to scream the Anesthesiologists kept reassuring me they would give me pain medication immediately following the baby's birth. The problem being the baby was so small and my uterus was large, filled with the amniotic fluids, placenta, umbilical cord, and somewhere was my baby. The team had to manipulate her down having to further open my incision. I was cut hip to hip.

Suddenly the tugging was over and there was a lot of noise. None made by a baby. I could not understand a word anyone was saying. There were loud noises and the clopping of shoes all around me.

As promised I was medicated right away making it even harder to understand what was happening. I knew the shadow sitting to my left was my husband, although I couldn't see him, I saw his shadow standing and felt the pressure on my arm as he stretched to look around.

The NICU team was rushing by us without even a glance of what was in their box attached to all the equipment they were pulling with it. My husband said he saw very little of the very little baby.

My surgery continued. I was to also have my tubes tied while they were in there.

I found out later that while trying to get the baby out two things happen. My placenta abrupted, now flooding my uterus and everywhere else with blood and when the Surgeons got the baby the umbilical cord severed leading to intense bleeding. I lost blood but the worst was for the baby. After they got all of the bleeding under control my tubes were tied and I was sown up.

I was taken to OB/GYN/PACU, at the late hour I had it all to myself, and my mom and the clergywoman came back to see me. My mom told my husband and I how worried she had been that the surgery went hours longer than it should have and no one would tell her a thing, then she saw a group of people running down the hall with an incubator. Machines on top and being pulled, people's hands inside the small openings, everyone doing a job running down the hall.

She knew then what that was as they passed her she says the one thing she saw was a baby's feet, to small to be a real baby, but feet up in the air.

CHAPTER 11

I am not better yet.

I did not recover easily from the surgery or the Preeclampsia. Preeclampsia is supposed to resolve, go away, after delivering the baby. Mine did not. I stayed in this hospital until November 14. I was discharged on large doses of blood pressure medication I had to take twice a day.

My son was at school when I got home four days after the baby's birth, but my daughter, Rana was out playing on our deck with my mom when we walked in. If Chris had not opened the door, she would have run through it! She ran into my arms and cried, we both cried. A similar happening when my son came home. I made him a promise that night that I would not go away again.

The next morning Chris took the kids to school and went to train his dog. I thought this would be ok, he was only 45 minutes away and my parents were to be around.

I had a plan. Get out of bed slowly, take my medication, and take a long over due shower. After I would call the NICU and check on the baby.

I still had a headache I did feel really awful but when I stood up, I had bursts of light in my eyes. I knew this wrong, I took my blood pressure and it was 200/140. I called Chris who was going to hurry home but would be awhile and I called my parents who assumed I was ok and they were on their way shopping but they were turning around to get to me.

Being a nurse (and using that pessimism I said I was so good at) I knew I was going to have a heart attack or stroke waiting for everyone so I called an ambulance. Arguing with the Paramedic that this was still preeclampsia and my blood pressure was truly this high-made things worse. She took my BP and had her EKG machine take my blood pressure but continued to tell me it had to be wrong-"Preeclampsia goes away".

The Emergency Room had no idea what to do with me. I spent nine hours there getting an assortment of Blood pressure medication and they debated amongst themselves if they should call my primary doctor or my GYN. Finally, they called both and yet again, my GYN came to my rescue, scolding them for taking so long to call him and then assuming my care.

I spent three days in the hospital while they got things under control, successfully braking CJs heart. I called twice a day to check on the baby and the nurses caring for me waited an hour after those calls to check my vital signs because there was never good news.

I stayed on blood pressure medication for four months. I probably have damage to my heart now but my doctors know all that happened with me and we will be ready should something in future happen to me. I hope.

CHAPTER 12

Heidi AKA Micro-preemie

One piece of advice: The NICU is overwhelming, your emotions are overwhelming. Get a notebook, diary, or journal, whatever and write down everything. Write down the things that you are told. Write down questions that pop into your head. Write down how you are feeling. This does not solve any of the problems but venting even on paper is venting and gives some relief! It also gives you something to look back on when hopefully your life has calmed down.

We were told before her birth the life of a micro-preemie is hard and no one knows the outcome should they survive. Their bodies are not developed and they just are not ready for the world. We were also told should she survive she would be in the hospital until at least her due date. Four months in the NICU to look forward to!

The NICU teams, doctors, nurses, respiratory therapists, were all there waiting when she was torn out of me. She was loosing a lot of blood with the severed umbilical cord, they clamped that quickly.

She was not breathing, immediately she was intubated and given Surfactant. Surfactant essentially keeps our lungs well oiled, so nothing sticks together and air can move freely, being born so early she had none and had to be given it artificially.

Her heart stopped beating seconds later. CPR was started before leaving the operating room. They successfully got her heart to start, very slowly, but beating. Off they went running to the NICU were she would live for the foreseeable future.

The team questimated her weight to be 1.5 pounds, 500 grams. This was done at the sonogram a few days prior to birth. Because of all the things that needed to be done to keep her alive and her fragile state weighing her was not an option for the time being.

The importance of this quested weight is for lifesaving medications. They knew her lungs would not be developed and her heart would not function properly on top of her tiny liver and kidneys that had to metabolize the medications.

She had blood work done and was soon given the first of a few dozen blood transfusions. Micro-preemies bone marrow is not developed enough to produce enough blood cells to keep the body alive.

She had several IVs placed for the known that one will soon fail. This turns out to be one of the baby's major problems.

I remember early in the morning after her birth, I was still on the Magnesium, in the labor and delivery unit for monitoring of my vital signs. One of the NICU doctors, an intern, and the baby's RN case manager D (also one of her many angels) came to my bedside.

Chris and my mom had left the hospital. I was not allowed visitors for a while to try to calm my blood pressure so I sent Chris and my mom to be with CJ and Rana. I was alone, unable to see, and feeling emotionally and physically like I had been hit by a truck.

The doctor told me that Heidi was born very premature at 25 weeks. Her body is not ready to live outside of me. She told me about the cardiac arrest in the delivery room, the blood transfusion, being on a ventilator to breath, and even being only hours old she had gone into full cardiac arrest again. Now the question was presented to me. Do you want to make your baby a DNR (Do not resuscitate)?

Being an Oncology and Hospice Nurse for the past nine years I completely understood the question, the need for the question, and myself have talked to many people of this choice.

At this point in time I was not a nurse; I was not in understanding of this question. This is my baby, my daughter, whose name is Heidi Elizabeth. I am not signing what would have been her death warrant. NO. I want all measures taken to save my baby. Should she become brain dead come and ask again but go and keep saving her, until that time comes.

I apparently got hysterical and had to be sedated further because of course my blood pressure went up, up, and up some more. One nurse called my husband and told him what happened and he needed to come, one nurse stayed right by side and talked to me calmly. This I remember, she rubbed my legs and held my hand and promised me that when the NICU staff had left me they would help my Heidi. She used her name, Heidi!

Over the next 72 hours of Heidi's life, she went into full cardiac arrest 3 times. Nevertheless, her nurse case manager stayed with her. Past her shift most of the time, she cleaned her up, stimulated her when her heart rate dropped (bradycardia), and took a picture of her to have sent to me.

This picture I let fool me. I knew she was small, I knew there were problems and new ones would develop. However, in this picture even with the ET tube (breathing tube) in her mouth she looked peaceful.

I saw her when she was 3 ½ days old. My husband had to take me in a wheelchair, he had seen her and told me about her, but I was not prepared.

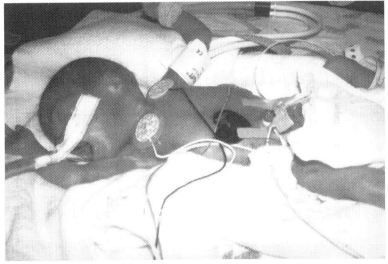

The first PICTURE

The NICU itself was slightly overwhelming but having done that part before I was ok.

Chris took me up to one the sinks for us to scrub up; I had no idea that my little Heidi was two feet right behind me. I had kept my head down coming in the NICU so I could not pay attention to everything, this was on purpose.

Then a nurse came up to us and spoke with Chris, they had met, this was Heidi's day nurse case manager and another one of her angels. C introduced herself to me and told me a little of Heidi's morning.

Her vital signs were low, she was having frequent bradycardias and apnea spells. Her blood counts were low and they were going to transfuse her when the blood was ready. An ultrasound of her brain was scheduled for that night.

Another fear with micro-preemies is because most are on ventilators having air pushed into their lungs and simply for the reason they are not supposed to be out of their moms, the babies have increase risk of brain bleeds.

These brain bleeds are classified as stages 1-4. One being minor and will heal itself to four being permanent brain injury leading to severe mental retardation or death. These bleeds can happen on one or both sides of the brain. They usually happen in the first month of life. Ultrasounds are performed every few days, in Heidi's case, for the first few weeks than every 3 weeks.

C told us D gave Heidi her first bath last night and that went as expected, with bradycardias and apneas, but she got through it. Heidi had a nice clean "bed" that was changed right after her bath.

When C came on duty that morning Heidi was weighed for the first official time and measured her. With the constant need of care as I said they were using a quested upon weight of 1.5 pounds. Now we have a true weight, she was 15 ounces and 12 inches long.

To give you a frame of reference this is the size of a Barbie doll in both weight and length. However now they could properly adjust her medications.

I was shocked, and then Chris turned me to face the side of this incubator behind the sink. It took me less then three seconds to peer into that big plastic box at that tiny baby to become hysterical. I sobbed uncontrollably for a good ten minutes.

The diaper they had on her, the smallest they make, literally went from her shoulders down, around, and up to the front of her shoulder. They had that folded down some because of all the wires and tubes and IV coming from her umbilical cord, but this was the diaper!

C gave me a towel and Chris whispered in my ear trying to calm me and finally some since of I HAD to do this kicked in and slowly I put myself back together.

I was unable to talk to anyone now, as I knew I would breakdown again but I faced my daughter and stared at her. She was tiny; I would not have known she was a living being had it not been for the forced breaths by the ventilator making her chest rise. She was on her stomach; it is easier for micro-preemies to breath on their stomachs. Her arms straight down to her sides her knees pushed up under her. The Endotracheal tube (ET) tube and tape to hold it in place took up most of her small head. In both arms and one foot were IVs also taking up most of the extremity and taped up well.

I could see pieces of the leads on her chest that told the monitors her vital signs and the golden heart telling another machine her temperature. Her skin was translucent. She had very little muscle so I could see her veins running up and down through her body. The fine thin skin covering her body wrapped around her bones giving the details of those bones.

C opened one of the small doors and encouraged me to touch her. Was I going to hurt her? She was so fragile. I reached in feeling the warm air and with the tip of one finger touched the palm of her hand. At that very moment she curled her tiny little fingers around the tip of my finger. This was my daughter, alive, and now I was ready to fight even harder for her!

About 15 minutes into our visit, she became over stimulated and had prolonged bradycardias and O2 destaturation (Oxygen level dropping low). Chris and I decided we should go. I was still very tired and in pain and needed to prepare myself for going home.

C gave us a list of personal things we could bring for Heidi. A blanket to cover her incubator from light, pictures (not that she could see them), and a stuffed animal that was in proportion to her to watch her grow.

Heidi was not being fed yet. She got IV fluids and nutrition through the IVs but nothing in her stomach. I was encouraged to pump and store my milk for them to use when it was time.

Another problem that can develop with micro-preemies is an intestinal infection called Necrotizing Enterocoloitis or NEC, this comes from food being introduce into the GI tract that is not fully formed, not having all the good bacteria needed for digestion, causing a part of the intestine to die and can open into the abdominal cavity causing sepsis.

The expectation for Heidi though is to grow at least ½ to 1 ounce a day. She will have a lot of trouble with this.

One unexpected thing was the tiny purple pacifier in her incubator. This pacifier looked like an accessory for a play baby doll. They wanted her to learn to suck. She did not have the sucking reflex, which would have developed in a few more weeks. The pacifier was still too big for her but it was the smallest one and she did try to use it!

CHAPTER 13

How can I leave my baby?

Knowing I would be unable to travel to see Heidi everyday it was decided the best times for me to call for an update were 9am and 9pm. I could call whenever I wanted of course but the nurse knew I would be calling at these times.

It is the hardest thing in the world to know you have to leave your baby but to also know I could not see her frequently was worse. I would be able to see her about three times a week for about five hours. See her; I was not able to have a lot of physical contact with her for months.

When I finally got home from the hospital the second time I sunk into a depression. I do not think it was specifically post partum but life seemed doomed for me.

Physically I felt slow and was in pain. Emotionally I was a train wreck. I had to try to smile and seem up beat for CJ and Rana. CJ understood his sister was very sick and would not be home for a very long time. Rana was just too young and did not understanding a thing. Not looking pregnant when I had Heidi Rana forgot there ever was a baby and got confused easily when I went to the hospital or someone would ask her how her sister was. "I don't have a sister

I have my ba." (ba is her nickname for CJ). This was her standard reply.

People called constantly, all with good intentions but I could not and did not talk to anyone. Chris my very optimistic husband just got upset when I was upset therefore upsetting me more.

I cried, just cried a lot. I was sad, I was angry to, but I was plain old textbook sad. My blood pressure was still up I was taking mega doses of medication and I felt like I would die at any moment. I did not want to die, I wanted to live, I wanted my baby to live, I want to watch all my children grow up and have their own children. I did not feel like this was even possible. Sometimes I just wanted to scream. Nothing specific and not at anyone but I wanted to scream. This is not fair. I know Life is not fair, but this really was not fair and my baby, my Heidi did not deserve this.

However even though I could not handle talking to people the pouring out of good will to my family was undeniably generous. The women at our church, after learning of our situation, started cooking. We had not been members long and did not know many people but that did not matter. They would deliver a full meal, salads, main courses, and dessert, for my family. No questions asked. Drop and run. I know everyone was curious and Heidi's godparents as well as our minister filled people in the best they could, but you always want to ask the person directly. They did not; they just made sure my family had a good meal each night. Some of the meals were also frozen for later use.

Liza, Heidi's godmother, would even take my children to Sunday School and other town events. They were given support even if they did not know it.

Therefore, I have to say that even though I could not handle people, people still handled me, thank god!

Then my thought process goes into the mode of what did I do, rather did not do. What if I fought my doctor harder when I knew my blood pressure was rising, what if I put myself on bed rest, what if I ate differently. All the what ifs I could think of but that did not change a thing now. Now I was the mom of three, the third a micro-preemie her life being spoken of by days by the doctors (Day of life 4, Day of life 5 ect).

My mom would literally drag me out of bed and to the hospital for the first few weeks. I called and checked on her but they also called me because something happened and they needed permission for another test. I did not want to go see her. If I saw her, if I touched her and she responded to me again, I would be more attached to this baby that most people thought had a very slim chance of survival. I know me and I know I would not be able to handle her death. I tried at one point to discuss arrangements with our minister (another angel) but he was not going to cross that road until we were there.

CHAPTER 14

Heidis fight.

After about 2 weeks of being forced to go and see her, I grew stronger, emotionally. I realized no matter what happens I was already so in love with her I had to spend what little time I could with her. I found that by looking at her picture and saying her name, calling her mine, or stating I am your mommy really helped. It sounds silly, but it helped me.

About this same time her breathing improved enough they decided to take out the breathing tube. The longer a baby is on a ventilator the harder it is to get them off and it does damage the lungs.

She was on CPAP now. CPAP is a mask that gives a continuous flow of oxygen to keep the airway open. She still desaturated but no more than when on the ventilator.

At one of these first visits where I was wanting and anxious to see her, she was 13 days old, I was told she was weighed that morning and gained!!!

Heidi was now 1 pound 4 ounces, her bradycardias were slightly worse over night though. However, this is the roller coaster we are now on for along time. I sat by her incubator and just watched her. She opened her eyes a little sometimes but the light, what little was reaching her, I guess it hurt.

She was also going to be closely monitored for ROP (Retinopathy of Prematurity). The eyes are not developed enough and the retinas can detach causing blindness. They can do a laser surgery to correct this before it happens so she has frequent eye exams. Her ROP by 18 weeks had maintained on the perimeters of might needing surgery but resolved on its own.

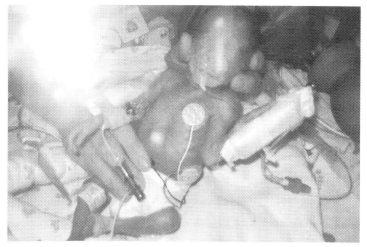

This is Heidi at 9 days old

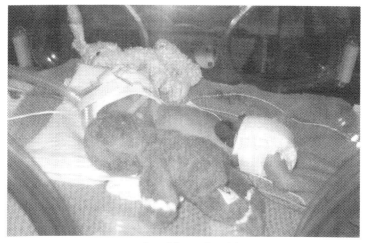

and at 13 weeks old

For the rest of November she was on and off CPAP and oxygen through a nasal canula. She still had desaturations into the 60% area and bradycardias into the 50s. But this is to be expected. I hate hearing this; I want to yell at everyone who tells me this is to be expected or this normal.

November 29 Chris and I went to see Heidi and took a purple blanket to cover her incubator and a handkerchief that I had kept against my skin. C had suggested this as well as tape recording our voices for Heidi to have.

C was thrilled when I told her I had the handkerchief for her. Immediately she came over and opened the incubator up. Chris and I just stared at her. C was gathering up all the tubes running to and from Heidi's body and all of sudden had her gathered up tubes in one hand and with me standing to her side turn to me and handed this tiny fragile baby to me, with tubes in my other hand.

Heidi's entire head and shoulders fit into C's hand her body resting perfectly along her forearm. We were shocked. Heidi did not move but she was in my arms, I could smell her baby smell, I could kiss her!

C took the handkerchief and spread it out were Heidi's head would be. Now it made even more sense, I could not be with her but I was with her (my scent).

It was exactly two minutes and suddenly all of her alarms started ringing. Her heart rate was down her breathing was shallow and her oxygen had dropped and she was getting cold. As quick as C had handed her to me she whisked her away and had her tucked back into the incubator.

I had not yet, but eventually came to learn that the slightest of stimulation would make her body react negatively. We covered the incubator with the blanket to make it dark and within minutes and with a little extra respiratory support the alarms became quiet again.

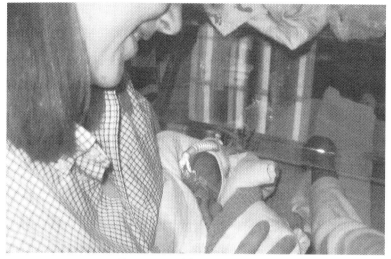

Picture Of The First Hold

After she settled it was time for her assessment, this meant blood pressure, temperature, and diaper change.

C got out everything and lined it up inside her incubator. She turned to me and said go ahead and take her temperature. I could not believe she was going to let me near Heidi again. I placed my hands in her incubator, lifted her arm, placed the thermometer under her arm and took her temperature. C wrote down the result and compared it to the reading that was continuous. I had taken my arms out and closed up the openings and she said I was not done, she needs her diaper changed. I was not so sure about this. C went around to the other side sticking her arms in and together we moved this fragile little baby around and changed her diaper. This was a good day despite not being able to hold her long.

This would be the last time I would get to hold her for almost a month, all two minutes.

The next day I woke up excited because my dad had to spend the day in the city and dropped me off at the hospital and I got to spend all day with her.

Heidi was having a bad day. Over night she had become septic. They were starting two antibiotics while they tried to pin down the cause. They attempted two spinal taps and could not get any fluid. She was also very anemic and was getting a blood transfusion.

I held her finger every now and then careful not to overly stimulate her and just watched her. She now weighs 1pound 10 oz. I thought this was good but they want her gaining one ounce a day and she is only gaining ¼ ounce a day.

During my visit a respiratory therapist was there changing her from CPAP to SiPAP because her breathing was worsening. They do not want to re-intubate her putting her back on the ventilator so they are going to try this. With this they can adjust her oxygen flow more freely and hope this help her. They start her on 5 liters of oxygen.

December

The 1st did not start off well. The lab work they did for the sepsis came back without an answer to the cause of her illness.

They started feeding her today. She is 21 days old and this is the first food for her little tummy. I am nervous, not excited, I just want this to work with her. They gave her my milk through an NG tube at 1 cc an hour. That is like a single drop on the palm of your hand. They hope to increase the amount every four hours as she tolerates it.

I am also worried because of all the blood pressure medication in my system. Some has to be getting in my milk but I am assured she will be ok. Assurance does not help now a days. I do not get as upset were as I mainly tune the words out. The next day her feeds were up to 4cc/hour and she weighs 1lb 12oz.

I call faithfully at 9am and 9pm and sometime in between. When my phone rings and caller ID displays the hospitals number, my heart literally skips a beat.

The afternoon of the 4th was one of these times. The doctor explained that Heidi's breathing even with the oxygen all the way up to 15 liters was not good. She was desaturating more and lower and the bradycardias were worsening too. They did an arterial blood count and it was bad.

The only way to help her now was to reintubate and put her back on the ventilator. I hope that on the ventilator her body can rest and grow.

The next day C told me she was at the end of a blood transfusion, and looked comfortable. However, at 2am, she aspirated a large amount of her feeding (the milk went into her lungs) and after they got her stabilized the feedings were stopped. She hoped after the Chest x rays came back they would restart the feedings. 1lb 14oz today.

On the 6th it snowed and was seventeen degrees. CJ and Rana had no school and the roads were covered in ice. My mom promised to get me to the hospital the next day and did.

Heidi was doing the same. Her feedings were restarted and up to 5cc/hour. She is officially 2 pounds!!

I brought a "My First Christmas" bib for her and the nurse found a tiny Christmas hat that had been on teddy bear and dressed Heidi up so I could take pictures. The bib which was for a newborn covered her like a blanket. But they did a wonder job and the breathing tube, NG tube, and IVS were not that visible. We then hung the bib from the outside of her incubator.

Picture Of Christmas

Her incubator was now decorated on the outside with a beautifully drawn picture of her name by D, the bib, and one of several blankets I had for her. On the inside was one of two handkerchiefs I kept there, a black and white picture of Heidi's brother, sister, mommy, and daddy, and a small picture CJ drew for her (His picture showed our house, CJ, Rana, mommy, and daddy standing outside, also with us was CJs version of Heidis incubator with a tiny stick figure inside). It was perfect!

I also had a small tape recorder of me reading the story Heidi, Rana singing songs, and CJ playing Christmas songs on the piano. The nurses played this throughout the days and night and even helped keep up on the battery changing.

By the 11th she was officially 940 grams or 2lbs 1oz. Her feedings are up to 6 cc/hour but her gallbladder is not functioning properly and she needs a medication to clear the "sludge" out.

Her ankles are in splints because her feet turn almost backwards. However one of the IVs in her foot was not watched and infiltrated (blood vessel breaks and the fluid leaks out under the skin) while in the splint. Her foot was triple the normal size and her toes looked like they were going burst.

She was also being started on a Diuretic because of all the fluid on her lungs and extremities. She would get this every 12 hours for months. She needed another blood transfusion.

On the flipside of all this bad, I was able to do Kangaroo Care (holding the baby skin to skin) with her. This was awesome. The nurse pinned her breathing tube to my shirt and positioned her on me and I just sat there. They laughed and had to remind me to breath. I only moved to kiss her and breath. This lasted one whole hour, I was in heaven.

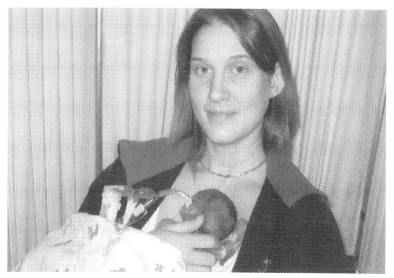

Picture Of Kangaroo Care

Dec. 13, just past 5am, my phone rings. Heidi is very ill. They think she has meningitis, she has a high fever and she did not tolerate her feedings over night so they took an x ray, which showed her bowel loops looked abnormal. They had already stopped her feedings and started more antibiotics but they needed permission for another spinal tap.

I called Chris at work to let him know then called my mom and she took me to be with Heidi. The first thing I saw shocked me, I had never seen it before. She was crying! No noise and not huge tears but tiny droplets falling slowly from the inside corners of her eyes. She was very still but curled her fingers up and out.

The Team was making rounds and the tests they did earlier were back. No meningitis but she had NEC in the lower right quadrant. NEC is classified two ways, medical and surgical. For now, she is classified as medical NEC and given four antibiotics as well as complete bowel rest (no food).

All I see now is the possibly of surgery that she probably will not survive that and my baby is in pain. I cannot do ANYTHING to help her! As a mom that is my job, to help my children, and I am completely useless. I stayed with her longer than normal but I began to feel bad (my blood pressure) and I needed to go home for my medication. My mom and I worked out for CJ to go to school and she would watch Rana at the hospital so I could be with my really sick baby.

As soon as I walked in her NICU room, C and other doctors and nurses surrounded me. My heart began to stutter. I could not even peek over them to try to see her incubator. They told me to prepare myself to see her.

I was introduced to some of the new people around me and they were the surgical team. They told me over night her stomach slowly began to distend. Her belly button has popped out and is large and she has red streaks over her abdomen. They were going to be following her case now. She had already had more x rays and blood work and they were waiting. They changed her to four different antibiotics and she was to have abdominal x rays every six hours.

She also went into respiratory distress and had to be bagged to aid her breathing. She had PICC line (a larger and longer IV, a smaller kind of central line) placed because her little veins keep bursting.

When I finally got to see her, they were not exaggerating. Her tummy was bigger than the rest of her. Her belly button was the size of a peach and she had red streaks running from it up her chest. She looked liked she wanted to scream. She was trying to open her mouth and just looked worse than I have ever seen her.

Now my nursing kicked in. I grabbed C and drug her over to the group of doctors that were now sitting down looking over charts. I demanded pain medication for my baby. The one thing I have always stood up for is the right to not be in pain and after everything she was going through and having done to her they were going to ease that pain.

We agreed on a low dose Fentanyl drip that the nurse could titrate (increase as needed). C got that done almost immediately and Heidi went to sleep. That was about all I could be thankful for at this moment but it was enough. I cannot hold her hand because she has an IV in each. I just stared at her, for hours.

By December 21st I all but moved in to the NICU, going home only at night. CJ and Rana needed me and I needed them. Chris is working like crazy trying to keep the roof over our heads and his parents are coming in town.

Heidi has slowly improved; her stomach although still distended no longer pulled so bad showing all her veins. She is getting big to. 2 lbs 8 oz, unfortunately some of that is water weight. Her toes on the foot that had the IV infiltrated a few weeks ago are now black. Plastic surgeons have been to see her. The Team told me they may have to amputate at least three toes but they were going to try some drug treatments first.

My in-laws came to the hospital and got to see their very tiny granddaughter for the first time. It was a quick meeting but at least they saw her in person. I was told before I left that evening they were going to try to take the breathing tube out. One good thing for her if she can do it.

All I want for Christmas is for my children to be healthy. I want the roller coast to come to an end for Heidi and for her to be a "feed and grower" (this is a classification of a baby who is low weight but healthy and just needs to feed and grow).

Rana is very sick; she has a severe cold that has triggered her asthma. She also has double ear infections. My little Rana has ear infections almost every month. She is going to be deaf if I cannot get that fixed. I was supposed to take her to be evaluated for PE tubes (ear tubes) back in the summer but I got sick and we know what has happened. Ranas need has been pushed aside and there is not a thing I can do for her right now. I feel like the worst mother ever!

Christmas Eve

Chris and I went to see Heidi. Usually I go when my mom takes me and Chris stops through on his way home from work to visit her but we usually cannot go together. It was a good thing. She looked beautiful today; D had given her a good bath and changed her bed, no breathing tube.

She had a newer nurse today and she wrapped Heidi up in layers and let me hold her. It only took 5 minutes for her to brady and desat and have to go back. That is when the nurse told us "she had her head ultrasound today and the bleeds were the same". WHAT??? She had brain bleeds this is one of my biggest fears and I never knew. We were never told she had bleeds. We were told from the beginning it was common and something they would watch for but never that it had happen.

Two hours later two doctors and the social worker came to us and apologized for the information "slipping through the cracks" that she had bilateral brain bleeds, stage two, but they have been there since the end of November and have not worsened. Chris and I both remained very quiet as I think our limits were coming to an end.

On the doctors behalf I understand they work a lot, and with these babies every day and this is one of the things that is very common. A stage 3 or 4 is permanent brain damage and she did not have that. BUT this is my baby and I need to know everything despite how repetitive or common it is!

Now I have yet another thing worry about. I thought we had escaped the brain being affected as they had told us it tends to happens right away and we were told nothing. Is my baby going to be mentally handicapped? How are we going to take care of her? I know people do, God bless them, but can I? I have not done a great job of taking care of her so far.

Now I know this was irrational thinking but then I blamed me and only me for pretty much everything this innocent baby was going through and if she was mentally handicapped to, I had completely failed the title of mom. I did not know how much one little body could take either. I have seen adults with much less die but she just keeps on going, how long can she last.

Her weight is down to 2 lbs 6 oz. Today they started feeding her again at 2cc every 4 hours.

Christmas Day

I stayed home with CJ and Rana and tried to have a normal Christmas for them. We opened presents and had dinner with their grandparents. I called a lot today. I tried not to bother the nurses but I just needed to. Chris and I are planning to sit down with the primary doctors and the social worker and discuss Heidi, from head to toe. I want to review everything that has happen since she arrived November 10th.

Chapter 15

Dec 27, 2007 "The meeting"

I recommend this for everyone, problems or not. One word: Communication. It is always good to occasionally get everyone together so everyone is on the same page.

As parents, we are so worried for our child we have tons of questions and forget to ask. Or we have the lack of knowledge to ask questions and therefore are never told. We also tend to put our complete faith in these doctors and nurses.

As for the Team, this is what they do. They care for these sick babies and it is almost automatic. They know there will be certain problems and there are things that will happen and what they need to do for those things. It gets easy to do your job even perfectly but forget that to that baby are scared and worried parents that do not have their knowledge.

I made Chris leave early this morning because I wanted to see Heidi. I got to hold her, for an hour! She did great. All of the bradycardias and desaturations she recovered from quickly. The only reason I put her back was I had to pump and have this meeting. The meeting went as planned. I brought a notebook with questions and a place to write any other information they gave me. It went as I expected.

So far for Heidi:

IVH (brain bleeds) - found 11/19, both sides, stage 2.

Apnea and bradycardias not worsening but not getting better off ventilator. Possibility of having to go on the ventilator again.

Anemia needing blood transfusions. This will continue until she has enough functioning bone marrow.

Gallbladder- even with medication is still not clearing, she is jaundice but while on the ventilator they can't give the meds so they are going to try again.

NEC- believed to be resolved.

Sepsis was caused by a severe, recurring UTI (we did not know this), and now they have the right antibiotic.

She has scarring of her lungs and will probably have chronic lung disease, asthma.

Eyes- Being followed as ordered for the retinopathy of prematurity she is at Zone 2 stage 0, (getting closer to needing surgery).

Her toes have responded to medical treatment except for her forth toe. It may have to be amputated.

I kept my nose in my notebook writing because I was on the verge of sobbing or yelling. That is all I do is cry, still. This baby cannot catch a break.

The 29th was a great day; in fact in my journal it started by Best Day Ever. C came jogging up to me as soon as I got to Heidi to report the head ultrasound they did last night showed her bleeds were completely resolved!! She had a normal healthy baby brain. YES!

She was also weighed and was now 1340 grams = 2 lbs 15 oz! Again, YES! Plastic Surgery was also in earlier and other than adding another cream, her toe stays! YES, YES, YES!

In addition, to make everything perfect I got to do Kangaroo Care for two hours. Heidi had a few desaturations and bradycardias but she recovered quickly. I hummed to her or we just sat quietly together, Heidi slept peacefully on my chest.

There were two gifts left in her drawer. They were beautiful dresses for next summer. The note was a picture of a beautiful baby, the notation was from the Foundation for this baby the parents had started, and she did not survive. This brought me out of the clouds and reminded the roller coaster had not come to a stop yet. However, I was feeling pretty darn good!

December 31 2007

The last day of the year. Could this be the last of, at least the major problems? Minor I can take but let my baby be done with the critical problems.

She gets more beautiful every time I see her now, less like an alien. I am not being mean but she did not look like a baby, not the baby you see on the street or on the TV or even one I have had before, she looked like an alien. That was changing; she is starting the New Year at 3 pounds!

January 1 2008, 12:03 AM

Chris is at work and CJ and Rana are in bed. I pumped my milk at 11 PM and decided to watch the ball drop. I have not done that in years.

The phone rings, my heart sped up so fast I thought I would have to go to the hospital. Heidi took another turn and not a good one. She is not breathing. She is desaturating to the 40% range and bradycardias almost as low. They wanted permission for another septic work up – blood work and spinal tap. I was told I should not come that she would be having tests and did not look well and I would not be able to be in the room with her. I called Chris at work and let him know.

Another thing I felt horrible for. Chris has never blamed me for what happen to Heidi. It was not my fault no matter how much I blamed myself but here he was working all the time away from his family. He is a Washington DC Firefighter and that to is a very stressful job as well as dangerous and here I am calling him to tell him what has happened to his baby. This is why I admire his optimism. I would not be able to function enough to keep going more or less protect and care for other people that certainly rarely ever thanked him. These men and women risk everything for people they do not know and the rare person ever looks back and just says thanks.

January 2, 3, and 4 were more of the same. Her breathing was a struggle. The respiratory therapist almost had to camp out next to her to bag her to aid in her breathing.

She also became a pincushion. She was losing IVs as soon as they got them running. Including her PICC line which she developed cellulitis (Infection under the skin) and it had to be removed. For three days they poked at her. She had most her head shaved, the beautiful hair that was just starting to grow, gone and replaced with IVs in her scalp. Besides looking bad, like horns when they infiltrated it was horrible. Finally a surgeon came and placed a jugular line (Large IV in the neck).

Her weight is down to 2lbs 9oz. On the 4th the let me see her and hold her. I was so scared, the line in her neck, even though its sutured in place, I felt it was going to get pulled out. Nevertheless, they wrapped her up and gave her to me. She was very alert and moving. I had never seen her like this, she had sticks all over, an infection in each arm and one leg from the sticks and I hoped she was not hurting, to bad. She is 55 days old.

Since Heidi's birth I have been pumping my milk. I breast fed my other two children and had to pump when CJ was in the NICU. One of things the memory blocks is the painfulness of pumping. Even when everything is lined up correctly and the suction is down it hurts, I do not care what anyone else says.

Since Heidi was so premature I had a lot of trouble with my milk. I pumped faithfully every two -3 hours. I had a portable pump for our trips to and from the hospital and I pumped at the hospital but I pumped very little milk.

Eventually I had to be put on a high dose of a medication that is for severe nausea but a side effect is increase milk production. This helped a little but I wish I could just breast feed and be done with pump. I know how much my milk helped my other two children so I was determined to do what I could for Heidi.

Finally, a few good days. On the 7th I came into the NICU to find her dressed and covered with a blanket. There was no heat on in her incubator. She looked beautiful and more real than ever.

C met me and took me over to look at her toe. It was normal! The black scab feel off during the night she had 10 perfect little toes. Her feedings are up again and C encouraged me to try to breast-feed her. That means I get to hold her!! For two hours I held her and she slept so peacefully. There was no breast-feeding happening today but to have her so peaceful and very few events was great.

The next day she was awake and found her way very easily. However as soon as she started to nurse my milk came in by the gallons and she choked. This leads to desaturations and bradycardias. We tried a few more times with the same results but she did it and that really mattered to me. Her feedings were increased again and her oxygen was turned down.

CHAPTER 16

Sibling visits

The NICU Heidi was born into was the highest level. There were many limitations to visitors and more for kids. The kids' part I didn't mind because I didn't want CJ and Rana to see something so small and hooked up to so much with all the machines around and making noises. However, Heidi, as of the 13th is now 3 lbs 14oz.

This NICU had one day a week between 4-6 pm, were siblings could come and visit their brother or sister who was in the NICU. They went to a small class that showed them what to expect. The NICU nurse who did this would show them some of the medical equipment, including the sounds they make and where they go, and had a doll made up like a baby in the NICU. There was also a short video. They got to put on their own little scrubs and were shown how to scrub up.

Only one child could go in at a time so the nurse teaching them about the NICU also did a craft and had a snack. Visit time was limited to 10 minutes per child.

January 13 I decided was the day for CJ and Rana to meet their baby sister. They were so excited. All they have ever seen is pictures and as I said earlier Rana would forget there even was a baby. We arrived at 4pm and they went through the little class.

It was decided CJ would go first. I walked him through the NICU and washed him up. He looked around at all the other babies with wonder and asked very good questions I answered the best I could. I turned him around and walked over to Heidi. He immediately knew her. He asked if he could touch her and C and I carefully moved her and her lines around so he could not pull anything and he stuck his hand right through the hole and held her hand. She was asleep but curled those long fingers around his. He did not want to leave. I took a picture of him next to her but since she is in a box it is hard to see her, but we know.

Now it was Ranas turn. She was extremely excited but the second we walked through the NICU doors she was frozen. The scene of boxes and cribs of babies hooked up to machines and alarms ringing just overwhelmed her. I did not force her in so we stood there for a minute. I pointed to were we had to go and she eventually, with her head down, walked with me. I got her washed up and turned to Heidi. Rana just started crying in turn started me crying. She asked me "what was that?" She did not want to stay so we left. She would be back tomorrow.

CHAPTER 17

Baptism

I thought for many weeks about having Heidi baptized. I really wanted a huge church service and celebration to follow but I had this gnawing feeling I should have her baptized now. Feeling guilty for not keeping her safe inside of me longer I decided she was going to be baptized at the hospital.

On January 14 2008 Heidi was baptized. Our minister who was a true support to us did the short service. Our minister had come to visit me at least twice that I remember before Heidi was born and sent clergy to sit with my mom during the birth and kept in contact with clergy, having them visit and pray for Heidi frequently.

The NICU allowed our minister, my mom, Chris, Rana, and I to crowd around her, with me holding her for the baptism. She did great and so did Rana. I thinking seeing Heidi out of the incubator and C had her dressed up nice after D gave her a good bath over the night, did Rana good. We also had C join us, as she is one of Heidi's many angels.

Her godparents, my friend who saved our lives at the beginning and her husband, were not able to attend and we will have a small service in the church after Heidi is home and well to include them. I made CJ go to school and he was very angry with me. To make the day better, Heidi was weighed that morning and she is 4 pounds!

Chapter 18

Step Down

On January 16 I was told when the doctors did their rounds that she was doing well and they now classified her as a "feeder and grower". I have been waiting so long to hear that phrase. I was so happy, but then they told me she was ready for step down NICU. It would be a few days maybe a week.

I knew this would happen but when the time did come it scared me. I knew everyone, there was an established routine, she could not leave.

The hospital she would go to now was the hospital given to me as the second choice of where to go when I was in our small hospital. It has a great reputation, it is closer so I could see Heidi more often, and it was out of the major city and a much less stressful drive.

On my drive home that afternoon, actually I was not even out of the city; the social worker was calling me for consent to transfer her tomorrow! I panicked, My baby being taken in an incubator with IVs, feeding tube and oxygen, all of her problems in an ambulance for a 30-minute ride, maybe more with bad weather and traffic.

At 730am on the 17th of January, in the middle of a snow storm, Heidi was taken to her new home, even though the stay was short.

This is a newer hospital; I will call it CH, with a new NICU. There was a playroom for kids with someone to watch them but more impressive is that siblings are allowed anytime. They still limit visitors but "the family" can be together.

My mom and both kids went with me to this new hospital, CH. Heidi had to go to their intake room were they did their own blood work and X rays and admission stuff. This took what seemed to be forever, but finally we were shown where to wash up and taken back to see her. CJ jumped right in, playing with her head! Not being rough but wanting to see her, she was awake and moving as much as she could so he took full advantage, stuck his hands in her box, and introduced himself as her big brother.

Rana was still a little scared but the set up at this NICU was much different and less intimidating so she settled in.

A member of the March of Dimes (anyone reading this please support this group!) came by and introduced themselves to me and gave each of my kids a bag with a stuffed animal a book, puzzle, coloring book, and crayons. Rana was now ok.

The nurse went over everything about their NICU which was very different from were we came and most importantly told me Heidi did well in transport, she slept and did not have a single episode. However this NICU being different they believed in complete low stimulation, so I was given back my tape recorder and the two beanie baby animals she had.

This hospitals doctors were concerned about the high dose of Lasix (Medication to decrease fluid) she has been getting. Her lungs are dry. The only thing swollen on her are her genitals. I had never seen anything like that but again I was told this was normal and will resolve. I really worried about this. She also over night started taking bottles instead of tube feedings. This is HUGE.

On the 24th Heidis godmother, Liza came to see her for the first time. Liza had a preemie to at 30 weeks gestation and Heidi was now as big as her baby was (who is now 6 years old and wonderfully perfect). Even though I know she was excited to see Heidi I also knew her old anxieties of what happened to her and her daughter were there but she did a great job hiding it. She even got to hold Heidi.

A few days later Chris finally got to go to the see her at the new hospital. Although CH is closer to our home it is nowhere near the way for Chris to stop through on his way home so he had not seen her or her new home.

It was kind of a let down because when we arrived Heidi was now back naked with only her diaper in a heated incubator. She started to have problems regulating her temperature again and was getting very cold. I guess though out of all the heart, lung, liver, and intestinal problems this one is much better. This hospital does not allow me to hold her, even bundled up though so I just hold her finger for short periods and look at her in her box.

By the 29th of January Heidi was as yellow as a lemon. She has always been somewhat jaundice but she was bright yellow now. All of her liver tests are extremely high and she is now losing weight again. The weight issue they attribute to my milk not being fatty enough so they are adding more calories into my milk then was already added and if that doesn't work they are going to give her formula. She is back and forth off needing warm air and holding her own. Again they tell me this is normal.

On the 31st she has another eye exam. Once again there is a new problem, the veins are strangulating (wrapping around each other). This will cause the retinas to detach. If there is no improvement by next week she will have to have emergency surgery on her eyes.

February

Its February, Heidi is almost 3 months old. I am now beginning to feel like she is not mine. On the 2nd I called to check on her and I heard this horrible screaming while the nurse spoke with me. She told me that screaming was Heidi. I could not believe it. Heidi slept the majority of the time and the little she was awake I had never so much as heard her coo. Lung damage, HA, she was screaming.

The nurse told me she was hungry so I called back later. I found out that she took her bottle and eat so fast, without problems, and wanted more. They also took her oxygen off, nothing to help her but herself, as a trial and two hours later she was still doing well. We did not think this would last but every minute helps her.

Over the next couple of days she had a lot of tests. The doctors believed her liver was damaged by the long-term use of TPN (the nutrition she got through and IV) and added Phenobarbital to her medications to hopefully help. The lowering of the liver enzymes is a side effect of this medication.

She had a bladder scan to see if her urine was refluxing (going up instead of down). She has been on prophylactic antibiotics for the UTI that made her septic before. That was normal.

She has nursed a few times and done well, but still needs follow up bottles. She is still cold, they cannot figure that one out.

Her Great Aunt Dorie and Uncle Bill came down from Pennsylvania to see her too. I think it was very shocking for them to see something so small even though she has tripled her birth weight. They were excited either way though.

February 7 I get that hated phone call. Heidi had taken a drastic turn for the worse. She was suddenly having severe desaturations and bradycardias again, back on oxygen.

Her stomach has become distended again. This made my heart go into my throat. I remember all too clearly the medical NEC she had and in the back of my mind this was it. She had escaped surgeries by narrow margins before but I just had this gut feeling there was no escaping this time. With her abdomen like this they had to stop her feedings and with lots of attempts got two IVs in.

They were doing x rays every three hours. Her abdomen showed lots of air but there appeared to be strictures (narrowing) in parts of her intestines. She was to have a CAT scan with contrast to try to see this better but that will not be until the eighth. The scan came back "looking positive" for strictures. Her liver is stabilizing at the same high markers but not coming down.

Chapter 19

DH

February 9, 2008 she was moved to the third NICU. Now in the need of surgery both for her intestines and she needs a large and stable IV called a central line. She had horns (IVs on both sides of her scalp) again. This hospital was 20 minutes further away but was a children's hospital, I will call it DH.

I had left CH about 10am on the 9th because she was having people of all kinds trying to get these IVs in her and I could not be with her. I was starting to break down and crying uncontrollably so I decided I needed my other children to hold. I was almost home when they called to tell me she was already en route to the new hospital, it was an emergency but they needed consent. I gave it and got directions to the new hospital. Chris wanted to stay with CJ and Rana and they wanted him so I picked my mom rather we switched driving places, I could no longer drive I was so upset and off we went.

When we got to DH I was very intimidated. It was a large facility, in a place I had never been, and when we made it to the NICU I felt brushed off. Looking back everyone was just busy caring for the sick babies, including mine.

After two hours a women comes to the waiting room. She introduces herself, she is Heidi's surgeon, Dr. S. First on the list of things to do is get that central line placed. Heidi was going to have to go back on the ventilator because of the medications (a paralytic drug) and morphine. The procedure she had hoped will not take long. I signed the consents and off she went.

Another two hours go by and finally Dr. S comes out to tell us first they had to give Heidi more medication because she really fought and second the line was in but she had to adjust it three times. Placement is confirmed by x ray, which takes awhile. We could now go see her.

We were taken through the same routine of where and how to wash up and taken to her to room. This made things more intimidating (at first), she had a private room, and all the babies did. They were monitored closely through large windows and monitor screens out of the rooms for all the staff to keep their eyes on.

Heidi would not wake up and looked horrible. This just could not possibly be happening. She has been fighting for over three months. We were almost to her/my due date. Now even though she is much bigger, 5 pounds 6 ounces, which is still fluid, she is still fighting to live.

We stayed until after 1 am and with no hope of her waking up and my crying myself into exhaustion we went home. She stayed on the ventilator for two days!

The day after she arrived at DH they did an upper and lower GI (looking at her intestinal tract from both ends) and a Barium enema and decided she was ok. They saw two small strictures but they did not think of them as harmful and her abdomen was of normal size so she was to start eating again.

On February 15, a week now, she has started to have large residuals (undigested food they are able to pull up through her feeding tube). X rays showed she still had contrast in her intestines. That should have long since been pooped out! She is getting suppositories than enemas every two hours until this contrast has past. By morning she had two small bowel movements but on x ray there was still a mass of contrast sitting just above her colon.

They tell me she is in a crib! I cannot even imagine that. I cannot see it either because my parents had to go out of town f or a few days and Chris has to work. Hearing everything that is happening the bad and the good and not being able to be with her is driving me crazy.

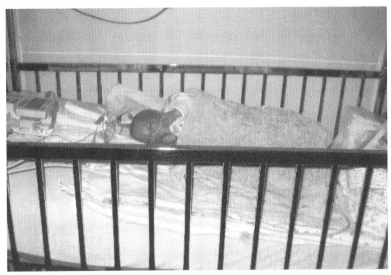

Picture of Heidi in crib

On the 16th Chris came home early and I took off. When I got to Heidi's room there was a crib. I walked in the room and there was a baby inside, my baby! A picture of her in a frame for Valentines Day sat on the dresser. Her nurse came in and told me if I was careful with all her lines I could hold her as much as I wanted. She was finally mine! As much as she could be anyway but I could pick her up, hug her, kiss her, and just get to know her.

I was to nurse when she was hungry and they would only bottle-feed her my milk when I was not there. She was very puffy all over but they were going to stop the fluids that night. Her jaundice has not changed and with the central line she had a huge catheter coming out of her chest with stitches in her neck. I can only pray she continues to tolerate the feedings and has a big bowel movement.

Our minister also came by today and talked for a while. I had a recliner next to her crib and for over five hours I held her and kissed her. They worked around me when they needed something and I resisted going to the bathroom. She strains so hard trying to poop. She grunts and turns purple and nothing not even gas. This cannot end well.

Over the next few days she was doing well, still not having big BMs but she was going a small amount and tolerating her feedings. I spent most days cuddling her. The doctors were even talking about discharging her. A person came and gave me her apnea monitor and taught me about it, one of the nurses gave the mandatory CPR class. Heidi gets to come home!

I let CJ take off school the day she was to come home and Chris and CJ and I went to DH. Only to find Heidi hooked back up to IVs. They had taken her central line out the night before because she was supposed to come home. Her abdomen was bigger than it had been at the first hospital. A doctor and nurse came in to tell us she was not coming home; I figured that out.

She was off feedings and they had to stick her several times for IVs. She was scheduled for another lower GI test tomorrow with tentative surgery and the surgeon would be in to talk to us.

She cried for 2 hours. She had to be in pain, I cannot stand it, I would take all of the pain for her and I cannot. I cried the whole way home and most of the night. CJ would come up to my room and just lay quietly beside me.

The only positive thing that happened today was when the nurse went to take her weight. I had been out of the room and walked in. As I have always done I said Hi Heidi. She turned her head and looked right at me making a cooing noise. I think she knows who I am. However, I do not think she will ever be mine.

Her tests came back positive for three strictures blocking part of her intestines completely. Surgery is Tuesday. This surgery means another central line placement, and then they have to open her abdomen just like my c-section only at the umbilical line. I know the post surgical pain that comes from having your abdomen cut open and I hate that she has to feel that.

Then there is the very real chance she will need an ostomy (the intestine is brought through an opening in the abdomen and bowel movements come out there into a bag). I hate this, I cry all the time, CJ is worried about me and he to thinks Heidi will never come home.

The nurses were having a hard time getting an IV and allowed me to help. I am very skilled in IVs and even though not encouraged for the sake of my baby and hospital policy they allowed it. She then had to have a tube put down her throat into her stomach and that is attached to suction. This is to completely empty her gut for surgery.

CHAPTER 20

Surgery

Chris and I went early to DH today, not to see Heidi but to sit down with the surgeon and anesthesiologists. Luckily we met in her room so I got to hold her hand as we spoke. The surgeon was Dr. S the same women who was there when Heidi first arrived and placed her first central line. I liked her that helped. She explained they were going in and removing the parts of the intestine that needed to come out, it would probably be necessary for an ostomy , she wanted to remove her appendix to avoid as many other abdominal surgeries that could arise in her future, and she would fix her large umbilical hernia on the way out.

I discussed my concerns with anesthesia and Heidi not tolerating it and was assured by those doctors they were on it. Now we had to wait.

The surgery took 3 hours. Finally Dr. S appeared and sat down in the waiting room with us. We were alone there. She said she had to remove two inches of Heidi's intestines; she then flushed her intestines with saline from the top to make sure they worked and Heidi had an extra large Bowel Movement. Shocking to her was not the size or the contrast but all of the meconium mixed in. Meconium is a babys first stool, its dark and sticky. Heidi is 4 months old she has had tons of stools but there it was.

With that part done she went to do the appendectomy and there was no appendix. We do not need it or use it. She called Heidi the evolved human. She fixed the hernia and patched her up using sutures, glue, and staples. What I did not catch when she was talking the part about flushing her intestines through and Heidi having the BM, I heard it but did not get it. NO ostomy!

March 1, Heidi has an infection, and she will not breathe on her own. She is so swollen she looks like a watermelon but is as yellow as a lemon. The plan is to first get her breathing! I was so scared of this and then get her eating.

This happened rather quickly. When I was getting ready to leave she just woke up! Woke up and went right to pulling at her breathing tube. I stayed awhile longer but I had to go. Chris had to go out of town for K9 training. I told the respiratory therapist and her nurse she was pulling at the tube and they needed to watch her but they told me she would not be able to pull it out and they had to wean her off the ventilator. I was in the parking lot when her nurse called and told me she pulled out her breathing tube and would be closely monitored.

I giggled a small giggle but a giggle, for the first time in a long time, she was stubborn and a fighter. She was going to do things on her terms. She is my daughter!

For the next nine days she ate increasing the amounts quickly. I was scared but I had full faith in Dr. S. She was doing great other than the jaundice. The infection cleared up, she was having regular BMs her fluid went down, and she really was doing well.

They started talking about discharge again. I tried not to be hopeful but they told me to bring in her car seat again so she could be fit tested. The monitor was left there from the first time we thought she was coming home, so I brought the seat. But no one was taking out the central line. One of her doctors told me they would take it out right before she went home, so there was not a repeat of last time.

I am trying not to be excited, she looked good before and look what happened. I was not telling CJ and Rana. Chris was supposed to be home the afternoon of the 10th and would pick the kids up from school so I could be at the hospital to bring Heidi home. That sentence did not even sound right to me. Heidi and home, it cannot happen, we have been at this for 18 weeks.

CHAPTER 21

Home?

March 10, 2008 - 18 weeks in the NICU

I arrived at the hospital at my normal 930am. Heidi was sleeping in her crib, everything the way it was last night. I got my recliner and was about to pick her up when her nurse came in to weigh her saying to me "today is the big day." I asked her if that was still the plan, for Heidi to come home? She told me it was more than a plan. A doctor would be in shortly to take out her central line and she had Heidi's discharge papers all ready.

I could not speak; I think I just stood there with my mouth hanging open. Then after a few minutes of her words sinking in and I began to internally panic. I was taking my baby home, in a matter of hours. Can I take her all by myself? No hospital? The room just began spinning. I took a few deep breaths and gathered myself when the nurse handed her to me and told me she weighed 6 lbs 10 oz and is 18 inches long.

I was scared; really scared but the joy I felt was also exhilarating to me. I talked to the doctors about follow up appointments and medications. Her liver was still not functioning and she needed two medications for that, and her specialist. She also needed to see her pediatrician tomorrow and that she would be seen frequently for weigh ins.

There is an injection called Synagist that is given monthly to decrease the risk of premature babys from developing RSV a respiratory virus from the common cold. She would get that today and I would have to schedule the next.

While all of this was going on a doctor had come in and removed Heidis central line. The nurse changed her diaper put her monitor on, and got her dressed in the winter clothes I brought in for the first time she was to go home.

Now here I was with my baby being put in her car seat, papers, and medications in hand. WOW. The nurse told me to go get my van and she would meet there with Heidi.

I pulled up and the nurse was there holding Heidi bundled up in her car seat. They had three rolled up blankets to give her enough support in the seat and it was cold out so she was covered well. I took her and the monitor with a soft thanks to her nurse and put her in my van.

I was almost numb in disbelief but also very hyperaware of everything. I had to get her home. It was a long drive and what do I do if her monitor starts going off. Luckily we made it home with out a peep from her or her monitor.

Waiting in the garage when we pulled in was Chris, he was about to go pick up CJ and Rana. He was shocked. I did not call anyone because I wanted to fully concentrate on the road. Chris started to open my door for me as he usually did but stopped when I hit the button to open up the passenger door. He could not believe his eyes and I was having trouble talking. He had to go and pick up CJ and Rana but he was having trouble moving away.

I got her in the house and she was sleeping so hard. I just stared at her she was home. Her monitor went off frequently after she woke up. She was easily stimulated enough (yes now she needs stimulation) that it did not go off for long.

I heard the door open and my kids call for me as they always do. I went to them and took them straight into the bathroom. They thought I was I crazy. I took off their coats rolled up their sleeves and washed their hands myself then got them into clean clothes. They kept asking me what I was doing and why," what is wrong with you mommy". I stayed quiet and led them into the family room.

They stopped in their tracks and also just stared at this baby in her car seat sleeping. Heidi spent a lot of time in her car seat for the few months because she breathed better.

Picture of Heidis arrival home

Shortly she woke up and was hungry, but also shocked I think by the look on her face. When she went to sleep she was in the place she had always known when she woke up everything was different. We all just oohed and awed that first evening but that night.

Nursing did not go very well. We only tried a hand full times in the past 18 weeks and she never truly got it. She would get frustrated very easily and then I to would end up frustrated. I know the importance breast milk and with needing everything my milk could provide for her I kept pumping.

She was used to bottles and that worked better for her but I would always start a feeding by nursing. She had to get a special formula for her liver and just to help give her a few more calories. Therefore, I guess in the end she got the best of everything. I continued with the partial nursing and pumping until she was a year old.

She also loved her pacifiers! After all they were putting one in her mouth before it really even fit in her mouth. However, she could not hold on to it. Her sucking was not hard enough to keep it in her mouth nor could she use her hands to put it there. We spent many frustrating days even weeks of trying to come up with ways to keep that pacifier in her mouth.

It was also frustrating for me because I have never liked pacifiers. CJ and Rana never used them. In fact when Rana was in the newborn nursery one of the nurses stuck one in her mouth and she spit it out using such force she got it out of the crib and on the floor.

The first few nights home were miserable! I have had two other kids I know about lack of sleep with infants especially when they first come home but this was a new kind of horrible. She cried all night long. I would nurse her; get her to sleep, just minutes later she was crying. She cried so hard she was making her monitor alarm and alarming me because she would turn very pretty shades of blue in between the crying spells. That was not good, and I could not calm her. I was her mother, I held her, I wrapped her, I walked her, and I dimmed the lights and turned the TV on for some background noise and she just cried. This happened every night for almost a week.

Suddenly, as everything happens with Heidi, she started sleeping waking only to eat, soon after sleeping through the night. Even though that sounds ideal the problem now was she slept so hard she had bradycardias and apneas frequently. These monitors are freakishly loud and even if I was not asleep it always startled me. Two dozen times a night I had to rub her back and move her a little to get her going again. This went on for months.

I did call the equipment company a few weeks in and they had set the magic numbers to high and they came to adjust that but she still had frequent events for months.

I have to include how obsessed I was with keeping as many germs possible away from her. First, the first morning she was home, after she ate and was asleep, I made a sign on 8 x 10 white paper and with red marker wrote as large as I could STOP. Beneath that in smaller but still big lettering, in red I wrote use hand sanitizer before coming in. I drew an arrow, which pointed to a very obvious table I had set up next to the door with four bottles of hand sanitizer. Next I hung a sign that simply stated, "If you are sick or think you could be getting sick go home do NOT come in." I also did not allow visitors and that lasted until June when I was confident the majority of cold and flu season was over, I still did not allow a lot of direct contact with Heidi.

When Chris came home from work he used hand sanitizer and went straight upstairs put his uniform in the wash (he is a city firefighter and exposed to a lot of people) and took a shower. When CJ and Rana came home from school they used hand sanitizer, went right into the bathroom, took off their uniforms, washed their hands and got dressed in clean clothes.

I laugh now but it was not funny then but the first week Heidi was home she did catch a cold and the person sick with her was me. It was scary though; she could not breathe well and spent every day for three days at the doctors. They tested her for RSV, if that came back positive she would have to go back to DH, our little hospital could not take of her. The test came back negative but we were there for three days and they just wanted to watch her because she did look bad, being yellow and a faint blue was not becoming for her. We do have the best pediatricians though. I would not trust the care of any of my kids to anyone other than them. Even the office staff is fabulous!

We were both better in about a week and she didn't need to go the hospital but I kept her sitting reclined but upright even at night to help her breath and I did a lot of suctioning and monitoring at home. After that I managed to keep her well and even kept the rest of the family well, there was a horrible respiratory virus that went around in July and again in September and no one in my family, but my mom got sick, and yes she was banned from my house.

We saw her pediatricians frequently for weigh ins and check ups. We also went to her liver doctor, a lot. The first 2 ½ months Heidi was home we had lots of tests. She had a day of radiology testing every couple of weeks, and the blood work that had to be done was terrible.

I have already said how bad Heidi's veins are well the blood work this doctor was doing required Heidi to go over three days because so much blood was needed then there was issue of even getting blood. She was a pincushion again. Her doctor believed she would need a liver transplant because her liver was so bad. This proved to me that even though we were out of the NICU we were not out of trouble.

I could feel her liver it was so swollen. All the radiology test came back normal except the look of butterfly shaped discs in her lower back which is the sign for a genetic autoimmune disorder that as far as we knew no one had. I have had spinal surgery so I know my discs are normal shaped but if this was to be the problem that was easy enough.

Heidi continued on a few medications and her formula was changed to a special one made for liver and metabolizing problems. The formula was so expensive ($50.00 a can), we had hospital bills starting to come in, and one of her medications was expensive. She was looking better after 2 months, hardly yellow at all. I took Heidi back for another follow up and her doctor looked at me and said she never wanted to see her again and laughed. All of the blood work and her test came back normal! She has never been normal.

We also in these next few months saw a cardiologist and nephrologists (kidney doctor). The cardiologist we spent the day with having tests done, his conclusion was her heart was perfect as far as the structure of her heart, and functioning valves, she just has to grow into her body. She was 5 months old now but in reality she was only supposed to be newborn, her body does not quite know how it is supposed to act. This showed true for many things. He was confident her bradycardias would decrease as she aged but he gave me all of his contact numbers and would see her for any concern I had.

The nephrologists we also spent a day with so tests could be done. The concern here was with all of the UTIs (urinary tract infections) she had and if all of the life saving medications she had been given especially those first few days of life had done injury to her kidneys. Luckily all of his test came back normal. She is different again however because her kidneys which should be shaped like kidney beans instead they are perfect circles. Everything that needed to be inside of them and their function was normal so I did not care if they were they were shaped like squares or triangles, they worked!

CJ and Rana are great with their baby sister. I thought there might be some resentment, especially from CJ with her home. They are both eager to help out and play with Heidi. CJ even changes the occasionally "pee pee" diaper. Rana is very careful even though it was hard for her at first to understand why the baby wasn't playing back with her, and when can she run around outside? Of course now with Heidi fully mobile they are really enjoying each other.

Let me clarify one thing. Yes, they love their little sister and everything I just stated but there are moments where I need to have two more of me. CJ and Rana do get jealous of the attention Heidi gets. I can take them to a movie, or sit on the floor with just the two of them but we have these "she's my mommy, no she was my mommy first" fights. CJ will even take Heidi off of my lap, carry her over to the most far away corner of the room, run, and jump on my lap while she walks back to me crying. Rana will just try to push herself between Heidi and me. However, I love that they all love me; I just wish I had more arms!

Chapter 22

Infants and Toddlers

Help, Maryland's Infant and Toddlers Program

Due to Heidi's great prematurity she was to be followed by the Maryland's Infant and Toddler program. This is federally funded and run through the state, each county caring for their children. She will be followed and given any help she needs until she is 3 years old. There are other programs after that if needed.

We were home a few days when I was first contacted by the nurse in charge for our county. She introduced her self and set up a time when she would come out to assess Heidi as well as an Occupational Therapist (OT) and Physical Therapist (PT). The next week they came.

Heidi slept through most of the visit but cooperated when the therapist wanted to play with her. She was to have nursing monthly at first and OT every 2 weeks. PT thought she was ok.

This program has been fantastic. Her nurse now only has to come every few months, she gets OT three times a month for development things like holding her cup and fine motor things, and she is starting speech therapy soon. I have taught Heidi some basic sign language as I did with Rana but Heidi needs some help in words. So her nurse had her evaluated and she gets help. It helps me to know there are so many people ready to help her.

Chapter 23

Development

Heidi has an adjusted age. This is based on the time she was born to her due date. She was born November 10 2007 and was not due until February 29, 2008.

Her adjusted age is 15 weeks less than her birth age so we say 4 months. For example she was 18 weeks old when she came home from the hospital, her adjusted age made her 3 weeks. Now she is 19 months old but adjusted she is 15 months old. On her growth chart she is small for her adjusted age but not on a chart at all for her actual age.

Developmentally this also applies. She is to do things for her adjusted age. She did not sit until she was 7 months old, she did not crawl until she was 13months, and she did not walk until she was 17 months. However, with her adjusted age taken into account she was ok.

She needed OT (Occupational Therapy) at first for her the movement of her arms. I had said before that when these babies are in the NICU they are kept on their tummies, it is the easiest way to breath. She still sleeps on her stomach, there was never "back to sleep" for her. Because of this and her abdominal surgery cutting through her muscles, she had no muscle strength in her chest or abdomen but instead had larger muscle in her back.

This was a problem because when she became emotional, happy or sad; her arms would jerk straight out to the sides. If you were holding her upright she fling backwards or if she was sitting in her seat her body would be pushed forward because her arms were stuck back.

With the help from her OT, exercises I did a few time a day, and her growing and starting to develop those muscles from using her arms. This slowly got better.

However when she now gets upset she will throw herself back like what used to happen automatically but will stop her head from hitting the ground and hope for the attention she used to get. It is quite a dramatic scene, maybe she will be an actress.

Her OT has stayed through all these months because she wants to make sure Heidi gets all of those milestones that happen rather quickly, sitting, crawling, and walking. Heidi also has trouble holding her cup. She just cannot seem to get it up while she is sitting, laying down she now does great.

No one knows how life will turn out. However, we do not know how our own lives are going to turn out. Heidi has the potential to have learning disabilities, as well as problems having her own children. There is not enough research following these survivors to know what to expect.

In my mind Heidi is a fighter, she has done things on her own time, she will be whoever she is meant to be. Whatever obstacles are in the future we will face them and get through them just as thought we would never get through the NICU, we did.

I also want to add again that the March of Dimes is a wonderful resource. They have all the statistics of preemies being born and survivals. How more babies are being born before 28 weeks now than 30 years ago? They also have parent blogs in many different categories, so if you are going through this right now there is someone else going through it to and you can talk with them.

CHAPTER 24

The unknown stress

Lastly I feel I should you warn of another stress that may have crossed your minds occasionally but now, in the first few weeks your home this next new stress happens. I have spoken with more and more moms who could not believe this happens, especially days after getting home.

HOSPITAL BILLS and not just the hospitals doctors bill separately and then we have medications and formula. Co pays and deductibles. Every one has their hands out and at the worst possible times!

I have never thought about socialized medicine but now that we have had to take a personal loan I have an appreciation for it. I see why people laugh at Americans. We have to pay for our babies, life saving medications, surgeries to prevent death. It is pretty funny.

We have an HMO. They have been good at paying the majority of the costs. Heidi also was entitled to Medicaid because of her micro-prematurity.

Let us face it though I was in the hospital, two different hospitals for a total of 11 days. I had to be flown to the other hospital and that hospital is a specialty and teaching hospital. I had a dozen different doctors, surgeons, and anesthesiologists. I also had emergency surgery.

Now lets talk Heidi, she was in three different Intensive Care Units, she had lots of equipment and medications, she had three surgeries, a dozen blood transfusions, tons of blood work, x rays, and other radiology testing, and all the different doctors to go with these things and for 18 weeks.

Then she came home, medical eqipment, medications, special formula, doctor visits, specialist doctor visits, testing.

Even after the insurances help, and even then they wouldn't pay for certain things we had debt piling up quickly! Heidis liver medication was not covered and each month cost me $70. I was on medications that I had to pay for, after insurance, and so was CJ for his asthma. Things that my family was taking before any of this extra stuff was added.

I will never regret having Heidi and I will always appreciate her battle for life and those that helped her but we will be paying for her for a long time.

Heidi is now almost 2 years old, time does fly! She is thriving, growing very quickly now, and keeping up with her siblings. She has developed a very strong personality which throughout her struggle is very understandable. She knows what she is going to do and she will do it on her terms –only.

We still have to follow up with specialists occasionally but she is on a good track.

Heidi will continue to be followed by the Infants and Toddlers program and receive all of the services she will need.

I have recovered completely now and I am off of all blood pressure medications. I still think back over everything we have gone through and I do still feel guilty every now and then.

I also still get emotional at times going through her baby book. All of "the firsts" were different for her or done by someone else. To ease my mind I remember her firsts will be much different then most of the people she will meet in life, making her more special.

We are still paying her medical bills but the end result in having her home, healthy and with us is worth every cent.

Resources:

March of Dimes – www.marchofdimes.com

This web site was very valuable to me. I heard stories of other babys and stories of their parents. The site also offers you information about preemies and resources for help.

I hope you can support this cause, even if you are unable to financially, word of mouth works to. March of Dimes works on getting the government support needed for taking care of these tiny ones and research to find causes and to follow them through life.

www.preemiesrus.com: This web site was where I found Heidis clothes during her stay in the NICU. They have special outfits that allow for IVs, quick access for the people caring for your baby. They have other items like journals specifically for preemies. Weight conversion charts (grams to pounds), day by day entries, everything to follow a NICU journey.

This is my Mothers Day picture.
May 10, 2009. Rana 5, Heidi 18 months, CJ 7.

About the Author.

Traci was born and raised in Southern Maryland. She joined her local Volunteer Fire Department at 16 years old and became an EMT (Emergency Medical Technician). This helped her confirm her decision to become a nurse.

She went through college and graduated with a degree in Nursing becoming a Registered Nurse.

She worked on an Oncology Unit in Northern Virginia and became certified in Chemotherapy, eventually running the outpatient depatment.

During this time she dated and married her husband Chris. They had grown up in the same area and his mother taught her in elementary school. They married and have their three beautiful children. CJ (Christopher Jr.), Rana, Heidi.

They currently reside in Chestertown, Maryland where Traci specialized in Hospice care prior to having Heidi. She hopes to one day resume that role, but mommy comes first.